"THE FIRS̶... ...EN-
TIC YET ... EX-
CELLENT ... HAT
LITTLE-KNOWN CUI...
—The New York Times ... Review

The Russians like to eat. They insist that their food be hearty, plentiful and immediately visible in all its splendor on the table.

From the lavish display of some dozen appetizers, to the substantial meal-in-itself soup, through the fish, meat or fowl course, to the tempting barrage of pastries, cakes and dumplings, the Russian meal is the only way to spend a long winter evening—or any evening!

THE RUSSIAN COOKBOOK

Barbara Norman has studied the food and cooking of the Soviet Union for many years. In **THE RUSSIAN COOKBOOK**, she takes the best dishes from each region and presents them in a simple, but elegant manner.

BARBARA NORMAN

THE
RUSSIAN
COOKBOOK

RECIPES FROM ARMENIA, AZERBAIDZHAN, BELORUSSIA, ESTONIA, GEORGIA, LATVIA, LITHUANIA, RUSSIA, TURKESTAN AND THE UKRAINE

A NATIONAL GENERAL COMPANY

THE RUSSIAN COOKBOOK
A Bantam Book

PRINTING HISTORY
Atheneum edition published 1967
Bantam edition published March 1970

Bantam Books are published by Bantam Books, Inc., a National
General company. Its trade-mark, consisting of the words "Bantam
Books" and the portrayal of a bantam, is registered in the United
States Patent Office and in other countries. Marca Registrada.
Bantam Books, Inc., 666 Fifth Avenue, New York, N.Y. 10019.

PRINTED IN THE UNITED STATES OF AMERICA

To the many people of many nationalities
who helped me so generously

CONTENTS

CHAPTER ONE

THE TEN CUISINES
OF RUSSIA

HOWEVER well fed they may be on other diets, Russians, after a time, feel a kind of emptiness only Russian food will fill. All other cooking eventually seems either too spare and lean or too fancy. And food is of great importance in the Russian's life. It was a featured pastime in the long idle days of the country aristocracy and landed proprietors. Meals and snacks were sometimes the only events of the day, and the supervision of the meals and the kitchen, root cellar, drying room, ice houses, and preserve-filled pantries was the main concern of the mistress of the house.

This preoccupation with food is so constantly reflected in classic Russian literature that I first thought of writing a Russian cookbook while translating Russian nineteenth-century fiction. Working at my typewriter with distracting images of pirozhky and other delicacies constantly evoked by the Russian text, I felt more and more sympathy for one of Chekhov's heroes who complained he had never been able to accomplish anything because the moment he set to work, his concentration was broken by thoughts of food—even the image of a boiled potato was enough to distract him for a day.

In Gogol's story of an elderly couple, "The Old World Landowners," the woman asks at every pause in the day—

1

when her husband wakes up from his after-dinner nap, when he gets out of his armchair after reading the morning mail, or if he wakes in the middle of the night— "How would you like a few little apple dumplings with sour cream?" If he shows no interest, she continues, suggesting mushroom fritters or hot meat pastries or poppyseed cakes until she breaks down his resistance and can patter contentedly to the kitchen to supervise the preparation.

She was not likely to run out of tempting suggestions. Russian food is far more varied than most people realize. The basic Slavic cuisine has been influenced by waves of foreign invasions from all directions and broadened by the adoption of dishes from all the nationalities absorbed into the U.S.S.R.

Russia today is a country of sixteen republics and an estimated 170 nationalities, many with their own languages, customs, and traditional cuisines. Not all, by any means, eat borshch, kasha, and Beef Stroganov. Borshch is unknown in the Caucasus, the home of shashlik, and even the way of making shashlik varies from one valley to another in the three Caucasian republics, Armenia, Georgia, and Azerbaidzhan. While northern Russians eat buckwheat kasha, a kind of baked cereal, Armenians serve a rice pilaf flavored with currants, cinnamon, and pine nuts. In Georgia, where rice will not grow on the steep mountain slopes, the pilaf is of cracked wheat. The sour cream and mushrooms of Beef Stroganov typify the Slavic north, while yogurt and dried mint are more common in the Caucasus, and hot red pepper is always on the table of the Uzbeks. In the east, there is distinctly Oriental flavor, and in the Baltic regions, a strong Scandinavian influence.

Local traditions are firmly rooted in the people, who have transplanted them wherever they went. All over America, Armenians are rolling feta-cheese stuffing in paper-thin layers of buttered dough, Lithuanians are eating their meat-stuffed pancakes with bacon, Belorussians are putting home-preserved beet greens in their borshch,

Russians from central Siberia are pouring sour cream and melted butter over bowlfuls of dumplings, Georgians are pounding walnuts with hot red peppers for sauce, and Estonians are assembling their rich, many-layered pastries. Restaurants unknown to the general public carry on Old Country traditions wherever émigrés of one nationality concentrate in numbers, and shops display the sausages, cheeses, spices, and other special ingredients of their native foods.

What, then, are the ten cuisines? First there are the Slavic cuisines of the three Russias: Little Russia (or the Ukraine), Belorussia, and Great Russia, the northern territory from the Urals to Leningrad. Next are the cuisines of the three Baltic nations, Lithuania, Latvia, and Estonia, whose origins are partially unknown, but not Slavic, and who have been more influenced by both Scandinavians and Germans than all the rest. To the south is the Caucasus, where, among thirty races, three distinct groups stand out in character and cuisine: the once independent countries of Armenia, Georgia, and Azerbaidzhan. The tenth and last is Turkestan, the Oriental land east of the Caspian and south of Siberia.

The Three Russias

Throughout most of Russia, the food is hearty, as you would expect in a country where the ground is frozen half the year. And Russians insist that food must not only be hearty, it must be plentiful. No matter how much I prepare for however few guests, my Russian husband is always afraid there will not be enough. My portions would impress the most impassive butcher and all my pans are hotel-size. But this is not unusual for Russians.

I recently noticed a handsome, long-handled brass pot, well over a foot in diameter, hanging in the kitchen of friends, who said they had brought it back from a trip to Russia. When they bought it, the Russians asked them why they wanted to carry such a useless object back to

America. The reply that they liked handsome cooking pots only brought another question, "But what will you do with such a small one?"

Russian Easter is a feast beside which Thanksgiving pales in quantity and variety, perhaps partly because Russians work up an appetite by fasting from daybreak till midnight despite the tantalizing aromas from the kitchen, where twenty or thirty festive dishes are being given the final touches after days of preparation. As if this were not enough to make them ravenous, Russians precede the Easter banquet by standing through an extremely long church service, whose midnight climax is a candlelight procession of the entire congregation around the church three times in the cold spring night. By the time they gather at the festal board, they are ready to surpass the justly fabled Russian appetite.

The table is covered with platters of food. Russians believe food should be not only copious, but visible at once. I shall always remember a newly arrived Russian woman's shocked description of the first formal dinner she attended in America: when the guests were led to the table, they found it set with empty plates without a morsel of food in sight anywhere! Russian dinner guests are instantly confronted by a display of zakusky (appetizers), whether in the dining room or at a buffet table set up in the living room. The zakusky will range from titbits that might be passed at a cocktail party (such as eggplant-caviar dip, pickled mushrooms, and hot meat pastries, or pirozhky) through a half-dozen other dishes requiring a plate, knife, and fork.

Zakusky are accompanied by a variety of vodkas, for Russians drink when they eat and eat when they drink. There might be orange-flavored vodka, lemon vodka, and zubrovka—vodka in which an herb of that name has been steeped. If you find vodka tasteless, try flavoring it with orange or lemon peel as Russians do (page 224). You can buy bottled zubrovka in America or even make your own, as one Russian émigré discovered to his delight. Carrying home a new broom from the local supermarket, he was enchanted by its smell. On closer examination, he made the happy discovery that it was, indeed, made not of straw but of zubrovka, or buffalo grass! Instead of sweeping the floor with it, he used it to flavor his vodka.

Zakusky are usually followed by soup. Soups play an important role: substantial soups of meat or fish and vegetables that would be a meal-in-one for many American families and in fact are a meal-in-one for poor Russians. Soups, in Russia, are never served alone; they are accompanied by a variety of foods so extensive that a separate chapter has been devoted to them. One soup, botvinia, is served with a whole fish, preferably salmon or sturgeon. Not all Russian soups are so luxuriously escorted to the table, but all have a garnish or side dish. There are iced soups as well as hot ones, for the bitter cold of winter is succeeded by intense heat in summer: the temperature rises above 85° everywhere in European Russia, even as far north as Arkhangelsk.

Because few areas of Russia have a long growing season for vegetables, the hardy cabbage and beetroot are staples of the north. Beets are the base of the popular soup, borshch, a Ukrainian discovery that is made in various ways throughout the Ukrainian, Belorussian, Russian, and Baltic republics. On pages 45–72, you will find seven versions of borshch. Cabbage appears both stuffed (page 165) and in stuffings (page 91). Sauerkraut has seen many a Russian through the winter when fresh vegetables were not available, and shchi, the soup even more popular than borshch, is made of either cabbage or sauerkraut or both (pages 55–59). Shchi may well be the first frozen food. Long before the frozen-food era, in the months when the bitter cold turned all the north into gigantic deep-freeze, Russians used to pack their sleighs with frozen lumps of shchi to be melted at the inns on long winter journeys.

Either fish or meat normally follows the soup course. Years ago, or at a feast today, you could expect both if not several of both. Although Russia has little ice-free coast, its many lakes and rivers are well stocked with fish, some of them species found only in Russia. Such luxuries as crayfish and caviar must once have been more common or cooks more extravagant, judging from some special sauces of the grand Russian cuisine that can hardly be reproduced today: a crayfish sauce whose recipe begins, "Take a hundred crayfish . . ." or a caviar sauce made entirely of crushed caviar—fresh Caspian caviar, of course.

Game is plentiful in the Russian forests and mountains: deer, grouse, partridge, hare, and wild duck. As in Scandinavian and German cooking, fruits are sometimes served with game, meat, fowl, and even fish. Cold-resistant fruits—apples, pears, cherries, plums, cranberries, and lingonberries—are used as vegetable substitutes as well as in desserts and pastries.

Mushrooms are very popular. Mushroom sauce is often served on fish, meat, or just plain boiled potatoes (page 171). It is surprising what a rich, dark mushroom sauce blended with a little sour cream can do for a boiled potato. Tasty mushrooms grow wild in quantity and variety, but wild ones are not sold commercially and trains leaving Moscow in the fall are packed with whole families going to gather them: fox mushrooms, birch mushrooms, and stump mushrooms. Cereals are used in place of vegetables to stuff meats, fowl, and fish, and are sometimes served as a main dish (pages 177–187).

As for vegetables, they play a minor part in Russian food unless you count potatoes. One Russian woman, asked what vegetables she remembered eating as a child in Russia, thought a long time before answering that occasionally, in the early summer, she used to eat a raw baby carrot straight out of the garden. The most popular Russian vegetable is the cucumber, particularly in the form of pickles. As pickles, it appears in the sauce variously prepared, but commonly known in Europe and America as "à la russe." This has, or ought to have, pickled cucumbers, mushrooms, capers, and pitted olives; it is a close relative of tartar sauce, which also calls for pickles. Cucumbers are eaten raw, too, anywhere and any time, just as we might eat a candy bar or an apple. When Chekhov described the governess in Act II of *The Cherry Orchard* as seated on a bench with a hunting rifle beside her, munching a cucumber, he was describing a scene typical of nineteenth-century Russian country life.

Russians do not go hungry when there is no meat. Their famous pancakes are prepared in so many ways that they have been given a separate chapter (see Chapter Seven). Bliny, or yeast pancakes, are a favorite dish, and the week before Lent (known as Maslyanitsa from maslo, the Russian word for butter) is marked by an orgy of bliny in melted butter. With sour cream, melted butter, and caviar or smoked salmon, bliny are a first course. They can be stuffed, rolled, dipped in egg and fried with butter to accompany soup (pages 103–107), or filled with applesauce or jam and covered with sour cream and sugar for dessert (pages 107–112). There is even a pancake pie: layers of pancakes stuffed with chopped meat and baked in the oven (page 111).

In the making of pastry, Russians are extraordinarily gifted. They bake it or deep-fry it, stuffed or unstuffed, in the form of pies, tartlets, turnovers, rolls, cakes, cookies, etc. Like shchi, the small stuffed pastries known as pirozhky were a staple food for nineteenth-century Russian travelers, who used to bring bagfuls of the satisfying morsels from home to last the journey. There are many dessert pastries, the best of which is the Vatrushka, a rich Russian cheese pie (page 208). There are cakes too: cumin cakes, poppy-seed cakes, walnut cakes, and the kulich that resembles coffee cake. There are cottage cheese dumplings, fritters, and jam dumplings. Berries and fruit jams are often used in making pastries and candies, and ices and ice creams are enormously popular.

GREAT RUSSIA

Great Russia, Belorussia, and the Ukraine are very closely related in culinary habits. Most of the internationally known dishes come from Great Russia, or what used to be known as Muscovy, the tsardom that expanded over the northern plains of European Russia to what is now Leningrad, south to the Black Sea to take in the Ukraine, and west across Belorussia. A variety of influences from all four directions swept over these plains in the form of invaders and a patchwork of alliances with other countries. From the south came the Turks; from the south and east, the Tartar lords of Turkestan; from the west, Poles; and from the north, Scandinavians.

The Scandinavian influence dates from the very beginning. What was to become the Russian kingdom of Muscovy was founded by a Norseman named Rurik on the banks of the Dnieper River in the ninth century, and the Swedes and Russians later fought for two centuries over Lithuania and other northern territories. It was probably from the Swedish smorgasbord that the Russians adopted their zakusky. You see the Nordic influence, too, in the lingonberries and cranberries served with meat and fish; in the variety of small pancakes with butter, cream, and a choice of delicacies; and in the liberal use of herring and crayfish.

Russian fruit soups are of Scandinavian and German origin. Dutch customs in food were imported by Peter the Great from Holland, where he kneaded dough with his own hands and learned to make cheese. German and Polish influence prevailed under Catherine the Great and Germanic dishes like duck with red cabbage became popular. All Russian cream and purée soups can be traced to the French.

In addition to the impact of foreign alliances and invasions, the growth of an affluent bourgeois society had its effect on the cuisine, particularly in Moscow and Leningrad. Cooking had probably remained fairly simple up to the time of bourgeois prosperity: borshch, shchi, and barley soups, cereals (kasha), and meats cooked in rudimentary ways. Under the guidance of an expanding Russian upper class, the cuisine was refined by the introduction of foreign ways. The grand dukes and rich merchants of Russia began to tour Europe and to bring

back chefs they liked from wherever they found them—
Baden-Baden, Paris, or other fashionable places. The
chefs proceeded to cook the foreign food according to
Russian tastes, resulting, as one Russian put it, in "a
French cuisine adapted to the Russian cornucopia con-
cept." It is probably because of this importation of
foreign chefs that most of the internationally known
dishes come from Great Russia. Some so-called Russian
dishes were invented by foreigners. The famous Salade
Russe (or Russian Salad), for example, was invented by
a Monsieur Olivier, chef under the last tsar, Nicolas II.
In Russia, it is known as Salade Olivier (page 39).

Perhaps another reason for the wider fame of Great
Russian cooking is that when Great Russian aristocrats
and bourgeois left Russia during the Revolution, a number of them went into the restaurant or catering business
because good food was one thing they knew about. Some
painstakingly learned to be or to instruct chefs; others
were given jobs that made use of their discerning palates
and, in some cases, the prestige of their names. One
Russian prince employed to taste sauces at a famous
French restaurant protested when the owner of the
restaurant began bringing favored clients through the
kitchens and pointing out "Prince X——, who tests our
sauces for us." That sort of public display, the prince
protested, was not part of his contract; however, he
added, he had no objection providing he was paid for it.
He ended with a handsome salary, but also with liver
trouble, which concluded his career as sauce taster.

LITTLE RUSSIA, OR THE UKRAINE

Some Ukrainian foods are curiously like popular
American dishes. The Ukraine is one of the few areas in
Europe in which corn on the cob is appreciated. Corn
breads, cornmeal puddings, and a kind of cornmeal mush
are popular in the western Ukraine, and Ukrainian
recipes for turkey with bread stuffing or with apples and
raisins read exactly like the American. These similarities

are exceptions, however, and Ukranian dishes resemble Russian rather than American cooking.

The fertility of the Ukraine, once known as the bread basket of Europe, naturally led to the development of a rich and varied cuisine, particularly in the geographically favored eastern part. An early rival of Muscovy for power, frequently invaded by either Muscovy or Poland and long dominated by the Tartars, the Ukraine has been subject to numerous culinary influences. Ukrainian cooking is primarily Slavic, closer to the Russian in the eastern part and to the Polish or Czech in the far west. Beets, cabbage, sauerkraut, cottage cheese, dumplings, bliny, and pirozhky—all these are popular in the Ukraine as well as Russia. It is sometimes hard to determine what Russia borrowed from the Ukraine and what the Ukraine borrowed from Russia, but there is general agreement that borshch originated in the Ukraine.

In contrast to Russians, Ukrainians like garlic—and garlic in quantity. They also eat more honey, more poppy seed, more pork, more lamb, and, particularly in the eastern part, a greater variety of vegetables, including the more southern varieties, such as peppers and eggplant. In the western Ukraine, the staples are corn and beets, and the borshch of this region is an all-beet soup, sometimes called Borshchok (page 52).

The great specialty of the Ukraine is baking. Stimulated by an abundance of wheat, eggs, and other dairy products, Ukrainian baking has become a highly developed art. Ukrainians claim the origin of baba, a tall cylindrical cake made of a delicate yeast dough requiring an almost unbelievable number of eggs in the old recipes: 60 eggs was standard. The cake is similar to the baba familiar in the West, where its shape has been somewhat changed and the dough simplified. Making the baba at Easter, when it is traditionally served, is the most important and perhaps the most demanding task of the Ukrainian housewife. If not properly handled, the dough is likely to fall at any moment, even after it is baked, and the preparation is time-consuming. Several old recipes begin: beat 4 dozen egg yolks and 6 egg whites for 1 hour . . .

Another cake baked for Ukrainian Easter, and only at Easter, is the paska (not to be confused with the Russian Easter cottage cheese dessert, Paskha). Ukrainian paska is a cake, not as tall as the baba and less rich. It is elaborately decorated and carried to the church to be blessed on Easter Sunday. The decorations, of dough of contrasting color, may be beautifully executed bunches of grapes or flocks of small birds, perching on top of the cake.

The wedding cake is another challenge to the Ukrainian housewife. One I saw was a cake with a tree of life made of dough springing from its center. Bearing apples and twined with blue periwinkles, the tree was gay as a maypole with a number of beautifully embroidered ribbons strung from its top to the edges of the cake. An unusual tradition connected with the cake gives it an even more important role in weddings than the American wedding cake. A large one, like the one described, is made by the bride's family. At the very beginning of the wedding feast, the cake is divided by the bride and her relatives, who eat it throughout the meal. On leaving the feast, bride and bridegroom repair to the bridegroom's family's house, where the new in-laws are waiting to share with the bride a similar but, I was told with emphasis, a very much smaller cake.

BELORUSSIA

Belorussia borders the Ukraine on the south, Poland on the west, and Lithuania, of which it was once part, on the north. It most resembles Lithuania in its cooking, but combines elements of all three with particular dishes of its own. A characteristic of Belorussian cooking, shared with Lithuanians, is the use of several kinds of meat in a single stew or soup. Feasts are celebrated with a variety of meats too: ham baked in rye dough, bacon, veal, and lamb make a typical wedding feast. Like Lithuanians,

Belorussians use fried diced bacon or salt pork as a topping on potatoes, potato dumplings, pancakes, and other dishes, but Belorussians have more extensive uses for salt pork. They make a soup of it with mushrooms; they lard meats with it, cook it with potatoes, and braise it with sauerkraut mixed with fresh cabbage.

Belorussians use fish more than Lithuanians. They dry them in a simple old process: soak overnight in salt water, leave in the sun 6 hours, cook in a low oven 15 minutes, then string through the tail and store in barrels. Parsley is the most popular Belorussian seasoning for stews, roasts, and stuffings. Beet greens are important in Belorussian Borshch (page 51) and are put up for the winter in many households. Mushrooms, dried or fresh, are a year-round essential.

The Three Baltic States

Latvia, Lithuania, and Estonia, Russia's long-coveted windows on the west, have combined the qualities of Slavic, Scandinavian, and German cooking to make a cuisine of their own. Lithuanian food has much in common with Ukrainian and Belorussian, for the old Lithuanian kingdom stretched south to the Black Sea centuries ago. Where the Lithuanians originally came from, no one is sure, but their language is related to Sanskrit. While the Lithuanian language has been mainly influenced by Russians, the Latvians, who are closely related to Lithuanians and whose language has the same roots, have been more subject to German influence. The Estonians, the northernmost of the three Baltic nations, are of Finno-Ugrian origin, like the Finns.

In the Lithuanian section of large cities in America, you will find stores selling Lithuanian products: strings of dried mushrooms imported from Lithuania and jars of mushrooms pickled or put up in salt water locally, rich butter cookies, Lithuanian sausages, dark rye bread, herring with mushrooms in oil, and the delicious Lithua-

nian white cheese, suris, that is something halfway
between cottage and cream cheese and is eaten four
ways: fresh or old (and stronger in flavor), and with or
without caraway seeds.

Lithuanian cooking is based on wholesome, rich ingredients such as milk, cream, eggs, butter, and potatoes.
These they vary in many ingenious ways without ever
disguising the natural flavor. Eggs and butter were never
spared in the old days. There were plenty of both in
every farmhouse, and plenty of pigs to fill the smokehouses with hams and sausages, and to provide bacon for
the fried-diced-bacon topping sprinkled over boiled
potatoes, potato pancakes, and other foods. Jellied pig's
feet is an old Lithuanian favorite, and suckling pig a
popular holiday dish. Strangely enough, although lard
must have always been plentiful, Lithuanians cook and
bake only with butter.

Throughout the Baltic, sour milk, fresh and thick, is
always on hand along with sour cream. The latter is
almost the only Baltic salad dressing; cooking and salad
oils are very little used. Baltic salads are of radishes,
cucumbers, tomatoes, sauerkraut, and pickled beets
seasoned with caraway seed and raw onions. The cooking vegetables are beets, carrots, and cabbage. As in
Russia, cabbage is the winter staple and is put up for
winter in huge quantities. An Estonian woman told me
she remembered shredding the cabbage with the planers
used to plane wood—a good way to fill the barrels
quickly. In Riga, Latvia, sauerkraut used to be sold in
paper cones at street stands and eaten in the streets as
are ice-cream bars in America. Caraway seed, believed
to benefit health and digestion, is often put in sauerkraut and even sauerkraut soups as well as breads and
cheeses. Other common seasonings are poppy seed
(particularly in Lithuania), bay leaves, allspice, dill, and
parsley.

Like their Scandinavian neighbors, all three Baltic
nations are fond of smoked or marinated eel. Estonians
near the sea used to hunt eels with forked sticks for fun

as we dig for clams at the seashore. Smoked eel is an essential party dish. Equally indispensable is a kind of salad with herring known by various names in the different regions (see Rossolye, page 38). Estonians and Latvians are particularly fond of kilky, or Kiel sprats, which are marinated whole with peppercorns, cleaned (a painstaking task with such small fishes), and put on bread with hard-boiled eggs. The Estonians like buffets with cold meats, herrings, smoked eel and salmon, sprats, and salads—all quite similar to the Swedish smorgasbord. And like the Scandinavians, all three Baltic nations are fond of goose stuffed with apples and prunes.

In Estonia, in particular, there are extraordinarily sweet berries: wild strawberries, large juicy blueberries, and a kind of cranberry known as klukva, larger and juicier than the American variety and particularly good in the Russian fruit pudding, kissel. Estonians also use the klukva to make a mildly alcoholic drink and a delicious ice cream. Their pastries were once famous: Riga (Latvia) and Tallinn (Estonia) used to have some of the greatest pastry shops in the world according to Russians who visited there before the Revolution. The chefs were French-trained and the pastries elaborate: cakes of twenty to thirty layers were not unusual.

The Caucasus

Here in the Caucasus, the land of kasha ends and the land of rice begins. The Caucasus has an eastern Mediterranean cuisine with flaky bakhlava pastries, lukhum stuffed with walnuts, stuffed grape leaves, yogurt soups sprinkled with mint, salad dressings with walnuts and pomegranate juice, and other southerly seasonings. All this has nothing in common with Slavic food, nor do the races of the Caucasus have anything in common with Slavs. Furthermore, through most of their history, they have been influenced by peoples south and east of them—

Greeks, Turks, Persians, and Central Asians—rather than by the Slavs of the north.

Here, pork and beef have given way to lamb. Gone are the butter and cottage cheese of the north along with mustard, horseradish, buckwheat, pancakes, and sauerkraut. Sour cream is replaced by a thick, creamy yogurt. Rye and barley are supplanted by wheat in the mountainous areas, rice in the lowlands. Beets, sorrel, and nettles disappear almost entirely. The common vegetables of the Caucasus are squash, zucchini, okra, artichokes, green peppers, pumpkins, and most important of all, eggplants, which are dried for winter use. Onions are essential to many dishes, and a wild onion with a garlic odor is used for marinades. Instead of the black bread and rye of the north, there is a thin, white, almost unleavened bread made with no shortening. Butter is almost eliminated, except in certain pastries, and never put on bread. It is replaced by olive oil in salads and stuffed vegetables, and by lamb fat in cooking. Walnuts, honey, currants, garlic, pine nuts, mint, coriander, cinnamon, rose water, and cumin seed prevail as seasonings.

ARMENIA

Spices play an important role in the Caucasus, particularly in Armenia. To walk into an Armenian grocery is to enjoy a unique olfactory experience. The tart, pungent odor of crushed barberry, the cool sweetness of dried mint, the musky darkness of cumin seed, the sour tang of dried apricot—these are some of the first sensations I was able to isolate from the multi-colored powders and dried pods filling the glass apothecary jars that lined the room. It is worth a visit just for the smells, but the eye has an equal feast on purple-black dried eggplants, shrunk to finger-size, rolls of lukhum stuffed with nuts, jars of every size of cracked wheat and every kind of dried bean, pea, and spice.

The Armenian cuisine is a highly refined and varied one that seems to encompass most of the best Near

Eastern cooking. Whether the Armenians originated the dishes and spread them in their many migrations through the Near East or whether they adopted the dishes from their neighbors and invaders is uncertain. What is certain is that the Armenian cuisine includes a large share of Near Eastern foods in exceptionally wide variety and often in original form. That the names of these dishes are frequently Turkish (dolma, halva, bakhlava) stems from the long Turkish occupation; Turkish names are used for some dishes in Greece, too, for the same reason. Today, part of Armenia is still under Turkish rule, while the rest of it, across the Russian border, constitutes the Soviet Republic of Armenia.

Unlike Russians, Armenians eat many vegetables, salads, and fruit. Fruit is eaten at any time of day. Salad sometimes constitutes a meal, and most meat dishes are stews combined with vegetables and known as misofs. Armenians are fond of stuffed vegetables (dolmas). They will stuff almost anything: tomatoes, cucumbers, zucchini, onions, melons, peppers, potatoes, artichokes, cabbage leaves, vine leaves, pumpkin, squash, quince, and apples. This passion for stuffing reaches its apex in a dish of assorted stuffed vegetables—small eggplants, peppers, tomatoes, apples, and quince, cooked together in a casserole and called echmiadzinskaya dolma. Most Armenian meat and vegetable dishes are served sprinkled with minced fresh herbs. The choice of herb is a matter of area preference: some regions favor dried mint, some dill, and some parsley.

Cheese is very popular. There are goat and yogurt cheeses and the feta cheese that is sold in America. Like fruit, cheese is eaten at any time of day: at breakfast, as a first course, and after a meal, with fruit. No matter what else is served for dinner, cheese, black olives, and assorted pickles (tushi) must be on the table from the beginning of the meal, and the cheese and olives stay to the end, even through dessert.

The meal often begins with a few hors d'oeuvres, known as mezaa. These include none of the dishes typical of Russian zakusky and are accompanied by the alcoholic beverage of the Middle East, raki, rather than vodka. Copious mezaa are always served at weddings and special feasts. A good platter of mezaa would include a hot flaky cheese or meat pastry; a few cold vine leaves or mussels stuffed with currants, pine nuts, and rice; cooked white beans in lemon and olive oil; pickled raw vegetables (or tushi); black olives; feta cheese cut in large cubes; thin, cracker-like Armenian bread; some chick-pea paste in which to dip it; and some thin slices of basterma (dried beef seasoned with hot peppers and fenugreek).

This course is followed by soup. If it is not chicken soup, which used to be considered a great delicacy because of the high cost of chicken, it would be a yogurt or vegetable soup. Yogurt soup, made with wheat, farina, or barley in addition to yogurt, is served cold with a sprinkling of powdered mint or hot with the addition of sautéed onion and meat.

Next would come chicken or lamb; lamb used to be the everyday dish, and it was lamb, not mutton. When I used the word "mutton" in talking with an Armenian chef, he looked at me very sternly and said, "No Armenian would eat mutton and lambs never grow into mutton in Armenia; they are eaten first." Therefore, it was lamb every day. But what a variety of ways to fix lamb! A distinct shashlik for every village, a dozen kinds of lamb stew enriched with egg yolk, stuffed meat balls, vegetables stuffed with lamb and rice, and even raw lamb patties, seasoned and sprinkled with chopped onion and herbs.

For dessert, Armenians offer fruit and cheese, or many-layered pastries with honey syrup and nut filling. Nuts grow in abundance in Armenia: almonds, walnuts, and pistachios. The first two are used for fillings and flavorings, especially in the honey pastries so typical of the Near East. Armenians eat many pistachios too, but not in prepared dishes—they simply eat them. As one Armenian put it, wherever you find two Armenians sitting and talking, you find a jar of pistachios.

GEORGIA

Quite distinct in its cooking is the small, mountainous and ancient nation of Georgia, known to history as early as the twelfth century B.C. and one of the oldest Christian nations. The sober Larousse dictionary bursts into enthusiasm in describing its inhabitants as "the most beautiful human race in the world."

The Georgians have been subject to the same invasions as their neighbors in the Caucasus and a number of their dishes are similar, but there is much that is uniquely Georgian and totally unlike that around them. As more than one Georgian has said to me, "Georgians are very proud people and do not like to be mixed up with anybody else." The survival of such distinctive tastes in food in an area so often overrun and ruled by outsiders shows that Georgians know how "not to be mixed up with anybody else."

One of the most characteristic features of the cooking is the use of walnuts in sauces—both pounded walnut paste and oil of walnut. Chicken in walnut sauce is probably the best-known Georgian dish, and walnut sauce, with its usual components of garlic, vinegar, hot red pepper, and coriander appears in many recipes (page 41). Georgians are extremely fond of peppery foods, of garlic, and of red beans, and have little use for sweets and pastries. In western Georgia, corn is very popular, whether in a kind of cornmeal mush or a corn bread. The latter is sometimes stuffed with Georgian cheese and served hot as one of a number of appetizers (Tchadi, page 30). Another unusual appetizer came to my attention when an American visitor to Georgia described eating a first course of twelve or thirteen "delicious grasses." I have since learned that Georgians, being extremely fond of fresh herbs (such as mint, parsley, tarragon, basil, watercress, etc.) serve them raw, without dressing, as a first course or part of one. Other items that might complete the first course are: cheese fried in butter with a little mint on top, spring onions, celery, red and black radishes, and Red Kidney Beans in Walnut Sauce (page 41). A typical second course would be suckling pig or long-simmered beef with various sauces, or perhaps shoulder of veal stuffed with rice, spices, and chopped meat. Another dish might be chicken sati, which calls for a fresh blossom of saffron, whole. The chicken might be followed by smoked sturgeon and topped with fruit. One of the most popular desserts apart from fruit is a hot bread filled with melted cheese (Khadja Puri, page 213).

AZERBAIDZHAN

Of the three Caucasian countries, Azerbaidzhan, which lies on the arid Caspian side of the isthmus, is the most closely related to Central Asia in its cooking. It is here that pilaf begins to dominate the menu. There are over a hundred Azerbaidzhani pilafs, all with rice and one or more other ingredients: meat, fish, vegetables, fruit, nuts, eggs, or just an herb, such as chopped dill. Several kinds of rice are grown in Azerbaidzhan, and some of the pilafs require a specific variety. For one of them, not even an Azerbaidzhani rice will do; it must be imported from Persia.

Like the Armenians, the Azerbaidzhanis make stuffed vegetables, meat balls, stews, and soups, but in their own manner. The soups are almost invariably lamb soups with onions, dried vegetables or potatoes, fresh vegetables, and seasonings. The soups are so nourishing and have so little liquid that they greatly resemble stews. Azerbaidzhani stews, on the other hand, are really braised dishes. Almost all recipes begin with cubed meat, sautéed with onion and then cooked slowly, covered, with a bit of bouillon. Often the dish is cooked until all moisture is gone. The recipes are varied by the addition of other vegetables such as eggplant, or fruits—quince, for example, or gora, the little undeveloped grapes left on the vine after the harvest.

Dried powdered plums, saffron infusions, and pomegranate seeds and juice are frequently used for seasoning. Lemon juice or vinegar is added to sauces or served in a pitcher on the side. Cinnamon, yogurt, and dried powdered barberry accompany many soups and meat dishes. In addition, almost all dishes are liberally sprinkled with minced fresh herbs.

Green vegetables and herbs grow in great variety through the mild Azerbaidzhani winters and are used even more liberally on soups and stews than in the Armenian cuisine. Sometimes, carrying the idea a step further, Azerbaidzhanis finish dishes with a topping of eggs beaten with minced herbs and baked in the oven for a few minutes. Whether the dish is vegetable or meat, this final touch makes it particularly attractive to both eye and palate. Because many of the herbs unfortunately have no equivalent here, we can only imagine the variety of flavors they imparted to the invariable lamb and do as Azerbaidzhanis in America do—use parsley, dill, and spinach leaves in default of other greens.

When I asked an Azerbaidzhani to name his country's best dish, he replied without hesitation: "Piti." Piti is a thick, aromatic lamb soup traditionally prepared in small, individual earthenware casseroles. It contains chick-peas, onions, potatoes, and a varying assortment of vegetables and seasonings, but the essential flavoring, kyurdyuk, is not to be had in America. Kyurdyuk, or lamb fat, is an important ingredient in Armenian, Azerbaidzhani, and Central Asian foods. This is no ordinary lamb fat; it is taken from under the tail of a certain species of lamb found in the areas that use kyurdyuk. These lambs have a very heavy tail, broad at the base, with as much as twenty pounds of fat under it. The fat is melted and used like butter for cooking; often it is added to soups at the last moment just as the French will add a dollop of fresh butter. Kyurdyuk is alternated with lean meat on shashlik skewers and even replaces meat in some stuffings. Outside the grazing area of these lambs, butter is the usual substitute, but the flavor is naturally not the same.

Azerbaidzhani stuffed vegetables are like the Armenian ones except for the occasional addition of pomegranate seeds in meat filling. Vine leaves are served with a sauce of crushed garlic mixed with sour milk or yogurt (page 175), also popular with roast and boiled meats. Like Armenians, Azerbaidzhanis like to make lamb meat balls, but theirs are unique: a single meat ball is enough for a family. The nakhchevan keufta weighs four to five pounds, and the zhidki keufta has a whole small chicken in the middle of it!

A taste for tart and sour foods extends to the dessert course, when dishes are served that would never be considered desserts in America, but are probably refreshing after a heavy stew or soup in the dry, hot Azerbaidzhani summer. Dovga (page 218), a cooked blend of yogurt, spinach, and dill is one of these.

Central Asia

Across the Caspian Sea, south of Siberia, lie the Soviet Central Asian republics, the former Turkestan. Here are Tashkent and Samarkand, from which the Golden Horde led by Genghis Khan's descendants rode to sack Eastern Europe and to rule most of Russia for over two centuries from the new Tartar capital on the Volga. Here Tamerlane built his brilliantly colored tile mosques in a city seen by only two Europeans in the course of over four hundred years. And here, until fifty years ago, was one of the most isolated kingdoms of the world, the fanatically secluded emirate of Bukhara.

The climate is dry. Once the basin of a huge inland sea, the country consists largely of plateaus and deserts with high mountains to the southeast. Much of it is subject to the extremes of temperature and sparse growth of deeply land-locked countries; temperatures down to minus 60° Fahrenheit have been recorded in the northern steppes. Yet the southern part, the beautiful Ferghana Valley, Alma Ata, and Tashkent have almost as temperate a climate as the Crimea. Grapes grow here, and melons,

apricots, peaches, cherries, and plums, all sweetened by
the hot and constant summer sun. One Turkmenian
melon is named after a rose for its taste and fragrance.
The Uzbeks take advantage of their sweet fruits by reduc-
ing them to thick syrups that they use in place of sugar
for candies.

The life of the fertile valleys, where irrigation supple-
ments the sparse rainfall, contrasts with that of the
steppes inhabited by nomad herdsmen, whose food consists largely of lamb, mutton, and horsemeat, and who
drink the fermented mare's milk known as kumiss, the
proverbial beverage of courage, merriment, and long life.
Often the shepherd's stove is a pit. Rice pilafs are said
to have originally been cooked in a pit. The meat, fat,
rice, onions, carrots, water, and salt were all tied up in a
sheepskin used as a sack, wool side out. A large hole was
dug in the ground, a fire built in it, and the sheepskin
was put on glowing coals, covered with sand or earth
except for a small escape hole for smoke. Cooked in an
hermetic enclosure over the slowly diminishing fire, the
rice came out dry with separate grains, as pilaf should. It
is impossible to maintain a gradually and evenly dropping
temperature in stove cooking, but many recipes from the
Near and Far East recommend leaving rice, once cooked,
tightly covered in a warm place or over a very low flame
for some time. These methods probably approximate
the effect of the dying pit fire.

Aside from shepherd's specialties from the steppes and
the use of horsemeat, Central Asian cooking has much
in common with Azerbaidzhani, particularly in the
southernmost and warmer parts of old Turkestan. As in
Azerbaidzhan, Central Asians use fruit in main dishes
and rice pilafs: apples, quince, apricots, and plums.
Unique to Central Asia, however, is the use of carrots in
pilafs. In Uzbekistan, carrots appear in almost every
Uzbek dish and in all pilafs except those with fruit.
Onions, turnips, and pumpkin complete the list of most
used vegetables. Central Asians use pumpkin in many
ways, even in dumplings, and they are fond of herbs,
sour cream, sour milk, garlic, and, particularly in

Uzbekistan, hot red pepper. Tomatoes, potatoes, cabbages, radishes, and other vegetables are comparatively new in the area and foreign to its traditional cuisine. They were not adopted without protest: local Moslem religious leaders denounced the potato as Satan's food and the tomato as a vegetable made of human blood.

While pilaf is the most important dish in the area, starches other than rice are popular too. Noodles are cooked with meat and vegetables much the way rice is, and dozens of flat breads, leavened and unleavened, accompany all meals. There are various stuffed pastries, large and small—eastern relatives of pirogs and pirozhky. The manty, large, sack-shaped dumplings filled with meat or pumpkin, are a common dish, akin to pelmeny.

Much cooking is done by steaming. Manty, instead of being boiled, are usually steamed in a special pot called

the mantykaskan. Steamed stews are cooked in a double pot not at all like our double boiler. The food is put in a small open vessel, entirely enclosed in a large one containing water and covered with a lid (Figure 1). This is a particularly delicious and effortless way of preparing a meal in one dish (see Azhabsanda, page 162). All you have to do is to cut up the ingredients and put them in the pot. No watching is needed; in fact, you are not suppose to remove the lid or touch the pot until time to eat the stew.

In contrast to this carefree procedure is another characteristic cooking technique: dividing and reuniting food. In numerous dishes, meat and vegetables are painstakingly cut into pieces the size of garden peas, fried in deep fat, and then joined together again. Pastries follow the same pattern. In chak-chak, hundreds of tiny balls of dough are rolled, cooked in deep fat, drained, and molded together in honey syrup.

COTTAGE CHEESE AND OTHER DISCOVERIES

There are new ideas as well as new recipes to be gleaned from a foreign cuisine, whether it is the discovery of an unfamiliar seasoning, a new technique of cooking (like Chinese stir-frying), or a new use for a common ingredient. In Russia (and Slavic cooking in general), the discovery for me was the versatility of cottage cheese. All diet-conscious Americans are aware of the protein value and low calorie count of cottage cheese, but so far, about all we have thought of doing with it is eating it with fruit or fruit salad. The Russians are far more imaginative. They bake it, fry it, boil it, and make dumplings with it. They fill pastries with it, stuff chicken breasts, and make supremely rich desserts like the tall white Paskha that always crowns the Russian Easter table. Of course, Russians are not interested in cottage cheese for dreary dietary purposes: they wrap it in a rich short pastry, drown it in butter, or sweeten it with sugar to make it fit for a banquet. If they eat it by itself, they put cream on it and perhaps a bit of cinnamon and sugar.

A better-known staple of all Slavic cooking is sour cream, which, particularly when freshly homemade (page 226) is a rich, thick, sweet cream, despite its name. In Russia it is called Smetana, not cream. There is hardly any kind of dish that sour cream will not improve. In Russia, it contributes to the meal from soup through dessert, from the dollop of sour cream in the borshch, sour cream in the accompanying meat pastry, sour cream and caviar on bliny, sour cream and horseradish sauce on boiled meat, and sour-cream salad dressing, to sour-cream pastries and sour cream on fresh berries for dessert. You would be as likely to find a Russian household without sour cream as an American one without milk.

An ingenious idea is the use of sugar to heighten flavor. Many Russian cooks add sugar and salt in equal quantities as a matter of course; if a soup needs one tablespoon of salt, one tablespoon of sugar goes in at the same time. These small amounts of sugar do not make dishes sweet, they merely accent the natural taste.

Another distinctive characteristic is the subtle combination of sweet and sour. Many Russian dishes require a certain tartness. Consider, for example, the two principal soups, shchi and borshch. In borshch, the sweetness of beets contrasts with the sourness of tomatoes and lemon, vinegar, or kvass. Sour shchi combines sauerkraut juice with sugar for contrast. The popular Russian dessert, kissel, is a tart fruit pudding served with sweet cream.

A highlight common to Slavic and Caucasian and Central Asian cooking is the imaginative use of chopped or ground meats. Some dishes are elaborate; others are almost as simple as hamburgers and much more interesting. Russian Kotlety are transformed by sour-cream pan gravy (page 151); Azerbaidzhani Tava Kebab by an omelet-and-herb topping (page 157). Lyulya Kebab is a shashlik of ground lamb (page 138), and Zrazy, ground meat rolled around mushroom and bacon stuffing, is a delicious and economical dish (page 150). And then there are raw meat patties and all the dumplings, pastries, vegetables, and even fruits stuffed with seasoned ground meat.

Some ideas can be taken from context and used to improve familiar dishes. The Armenian way of adding lemon juice and egg yolks to flavor and thicken meat sauces and soups can transform a plain chicken stew or a canned bouillon. Sprinkling chopped fresh herbs on a warmed-over meat stew will revive both its taste and appearance. Kasha or wheat or rice pilaf can be substituted for bread in stuffings for fowl and meats. Stews of all sorts can be cooked with almost no watching in the Uzbek double pot. Using leftovers in dumplings, pancake stuffings, and meat balls can lead to new discoveries. But let us start with the classic recipes.

CHAPTER TWO

ZAKUSKY AND OTHER APPETIZERS

ZAKUSITS means to have a snack, and zakusky are the hot and cold appetizers Russians serve before going on to the main part of the meal. Zakusky should be varied—the more varied, the better—and a good collection of zakusky can make a meal. Therein lies the danger. Because most Americans do not have the seven-league appetites of Russians (or if they do, they are probably dieting), a copious spread of zakusky prior to a full-course dinner is not to be recommended. If the zakusky are good, no one eats dinner; if not, no one eats the zakusky, which is equally disappointing. A full Russian selection of zakusky makes a full American buffet dinner and should be presented as such. Otherwise, it is best to select a few zakusky to be served at the table as a first course as Russians do in an informal family meal, or to pass two or three zakusky with drinks before dinner.

At a formal Russian meal, the zakusky are served in the living room or reception room. A table covered with a cloth is set with plates, forks, knives, vodka glasses, various kinds of vodka, black bread, white rolls, butter, and dishes containing all sorts of delicacies. The guests help themselves and usually eat standing.

In addition to food prepared at home, Russians fill the dishes with smoked fish (sturgeon, salmon, and eel), herring in marinades and sauces, anchovies, sprats, caviar, sausages, liver pâté, cold meats and fowl, olives, and pickles. Some of the zakusky that used to have to be made at home can now be bought in cans: stuffed vine leaves, stuffed peppers, and pickled vegetables of all kinds are sold in specialty stores in America as well as in Russia.

Prepared cold dishes might include salads of cooked vegetables with fish (Rossolye) or meats (Salade Olivier), radishes in sour cream, or cucumbers in sour cream, all described in the following chapter. Fish in aspic (page 114) is sometimes cut in small cubes and presented on a zakusky plate with a bit of mustard or horseradish sauce on each cube. Among the hot dishes, you might find small pirozhky with various stuffings (pages 89–96) and little Bitky, or meat balls, on toothpicks (page 29). Some Caucasian dishes, also included in this chapter, have become popular zakusky in northern Russia: white-bean salad and eggplant caviar, for example.

While neither Armenians nor Georgians serve Russian-style zakusky, both have their own selections of assorted hors d'oeuvres. Some delicious specialties from these areas, such as Armenian hot cheese pastries, or beoregs, and Georgian red-bean salad will be found in this chapter too. A large beoreg served alone makes a first course. Rossolye, Salade Olivier, and fish in aspic also constitute first courses on their own.

CHEE KEUFTA

Armenian Raw Lamb Patties

This Armenian version of Tartar beefsteak can be served as a first course or one of many appetizers.

SERVINGS: 6

>   *1 recipe for exterior of Harput Keufta (page 152)*
>   *ground black pepper to taste*
>   *garnish: 1 medium onion, ½ bunch parsley, 1 small green pepper, 2 tomatoes*

Prepare mixture of wheat and meat as for exterior of Harput Keufta, and knead mixture with black pepper. Scoop a small handful into the palm of your hand, make a fist, squeezing the mixture lightly, and drop it onto a serving platter. This presses the mixture into a long piece, marked with indentations from the fingers. Prepare all the patties in the same way. Garnish them with minced onion, parsley, and pepper, and the tomatoes cut in eighths.

BITKY

Russian Meat Balls

Made into miniature round balls, served 1 to a toothpick, bitky make good appetizers.

SERVINGS: 1 doz. tiny meatballs

> 2 slices white bread
> ¾ cup milk
> ½ lb. ground chuck
> salt and ground black pepper to taste
> 1 egg yolk
> flour for dusting
> 1 egg, beaten
> ¼ cup fine dry bread crumbs
> 2–3 Tb butter

Remove crusts from bread and soak white part in milk ½ hour. Squeeze the bread thoroughly and mix it with the meat, salt, pepper, and egg yolk. With wet hands, form tiny meat balls (bite-size). Roll them in flour, beaten egg, and bread crumbs, in that order. Fry in hot butter until well browned on all sides.

TCHADI

Georgian Corn Bread

Tchadi is a solid, satisfying peasant corn bread. In Georgia, it is stuffed with either feta cheese or smoked bacon and served as one of several appetizers composing a first course. Tchadi is quickly made and only eaten hot; once cooled, it is no longer good.

SERVINGS: 6–8

> 3 cups fine cornmeal*
> 3 cups water
> 1 tsp salt
> 1 tsp bacon grease
> 6 Tb feta cheese, cut in small bits

Set oven to 450°. Sift cornmeal and beat with water and salt until it is the consistency of lightly whipped cream. Rub a large square baking pan with bacon grease. Divide cornmeal dough in half. With wet hands pat a thin, even layer into shape in the pan. Sprinkle the top with bits of feta cheese, and press remaining cornmeal into a second layer over it. (Although the dough crumbles and could never be rolled out or cut, it is easy to mold into shape.)

Bake in top part of 450° oven 25–30 minutes, or until it has a firm, lightly browned crust. Serve at once.

BEOREGS

Armenian Stuffed Pastries

These delicious many-layered pastries stuffed with savory fillings can be used as a first course or for appe-

---

* If the germ has been removed from the cornmeal, use 2½ cups cornmeal and ½ cup wheat flour. Whole cornmeal is sold in health food stores.

tizers. Even as appetizers, they are best served alone because they are so delectable that all other titbits, however good, are eclipsed.

Beoregs are easy to make with the filo dough (also known as strudel dough) that is sold packaged and ready to use. This dough, wrapped in cellophane in long, narrow boxes, is available almost everywhere in the United States, by mail order if not in local stores.* The dough will keep 4 or 5 months in a freezer, about 10 days in the refrigerator.

Filo dough is made of mere flour, water, and salt, but this very ordinary mixture is stretched and pulled into huge, thin sheets in a process spectacular to watch. I saw it made for the first time at the Constantinople Oriental Pastry Shop on Eighth Avenue in New York, where I was permitted to observe the preparation of the dough from beginning to end.

In the bare back room of the shop, two men and two young women, working to Greek music from a phonograph that occasionally becomes stuck on three notes, make 250 lbs. of filo dough a day. The equipment consists of three tables about the size and height of billiard tables, an electric mixer, a long shelf, a dryer, and numerous large white sheets of sacking. The process is long, rhythmic, and repetitive, like the music that accompanies it.

The first step is to add flour to water (along with about ½ lb. salt for every 35–40 lbs. of dough) until the mixture is the consistency of a hard bread dough. When worked, the dough softens and becomes stringy and elastic. It is then cut in sections, formed into balls, and rolled out, with the aid of cornstarch (not flour), into giant pancakes, 15 or 16 inches across. These are left to rest for about an hour before being "thrown."

Throwing is the technical term for stretching the filo dough and the extraordinary part of the process. It is

---

* Greek, Armenian, and Near Eastern groceries carry it, as do many gourmet shops. Some supermarkets now stock it, and a mail order address is given on page 236 of the Appendix.

the men who do the stretching. Each picks up one of the pancakes and drapes it over crooked elbows, held out stiffly, chest high. Raising first the right, then the left elbow in a sort of jig, he makes the pancake rotate, and as it turns, its size increases. Gradually the pancake grows until it is only by holding his elbows very high that the man keeps it from touching the floor. At this moment, he throws it onto one of the large tables over which one of the young women has spread a coarse sheet sprinkled with cornstarch. Walking around the table, the man pulls on the edges of the dough to stretch it to cover the table completely. He is followed by the young woman with a knife. Holding the dough down with one hand, she slices it off even with the table edges. The scraps are tossed into a large container of water to be soaked and used again in the next batch of dough.

I watched this process being repeated over and over. The alternate layers of stretched filo dough and coarse sheets began to pile high on the two large tables. After a few minutes, I noticed that some of the sheets were taken from the left side of the room, where the dough mixer was, and others from the right, where the dryer was located. The owner explained that warm sheets from the dryer or cool ones from the lefthand side of the room are chosen according to the fluctuating consistency of the dough. The older and more experienced of the two men would occasionally lift the sheets of dough and cloth and thumb through them to determine which temperature the next sheet should be.

When the entire stack of dough pancakes had been stretched, worked, and placed on the tables, the process of brushing began. The middle table was cleared. The women got out long-handled brushes with long soft bristles and 2 bowls filled with cornstarch. As the men lifted each translucent sheet of stretched dough from the end table to the middle one, the women proceeded to brush the cornstarch over it and then lift it to the third table, where the finished dough is stacked throughout the day. At the end of the day, all the sheets of dough

on that table are cut and packaged, and the day's work—
250 lbs. of filo dough—is completed.

ROLLING BEOREGS

The explanation that follows is long, but it need only
be read once in order to learn the method. Thereafter,
rolling beoregs will be as automatic as cutting cookies.

If the filo dough is frozen, let it defrost 20 hours before
use. If it has been stored in the refrigerator, it need be
taken out only 1 hour in advance. Keep whatever portion
of the dough you are not going to use in cellophane or
wax paper to prevent its drying out. Dried filo dough
flakes, requires more butter to make it flexible, and is
generally hard to handle.

Before starting to roll the beoregs, set the oven at 300°,
clear a large flat surface, and have ready a pot of melted
butter, a pastry brush, a tablespoon, a bowl of beoreg
filling (pages 34–35), and a buttered cookie sheet.

If you are serving beoregs as a first course, you will
want to make a single large one for each person. For
each beoreg, spread 1 sheet of filo dough out flat and
brush it with melted butter. Fold it lengthwise, in thirds,
bringing the bottom third over the center and the top
third over that (Figure 1). Brush with melted butter
each time you fold.

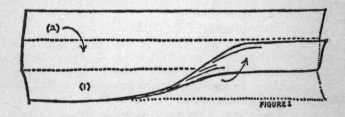

FIGURE 1

Put 1 scant Tb stuffing in a compact heap on the lower
righthand section of the folded dough (Figure 2). Fold

a triangular-shaped piece of dough (A) over the stuffing (B). Keep your index finger on the pivot angle of the

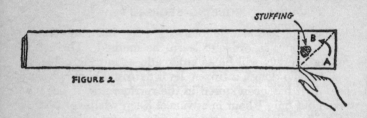

FIGURE 2.

triangle as shown in the diagram. Put another scant Tb of stuffing in the upper righthand section of the unfolded dough, and fold the triangle (B) over it. Continue in the same manner, always keeping your index finger on the pivot angle of the triangle to seal in the stuffing, and always brushing each newly exposed surface with melted butter. When the entire strip of dough is folded into a triangle, tamp down any loose flakes with the aid of melted butter and place the beoreg, open side down, on a buttered cookie sheet. Repeat the process for all other beoregs.

NOTE: Appetizer beoregs should be bite-size. Cut large filo sheets in 4 and use 1 scant tsp filling or less instead of 1 Tb. Roll as described above.

MEAT BEOREGS

The filling can be prepared a day in advance very successfully. While it is made entirely from lamb in Armenia, beef is sometimes substituted in the U.S. At the Dardanelles Restaurant in New York, which contributed the following recipe, it is made with half lamb, half beef.

SERVINGS: 10–12 regular beoregs or 4 doz. cocktail beoregs

½ lb. fatty ground beef
½ lb. fatty ground lamb
2 Tb butter
1 cup minced onion
¼ cup minced green pepper
2 Tb chopped fresh parsley
1 Tb chopped fresh basil (or 1 tsp dried basil)
¼ cup pine nuts (can be omitted if not available)
salt and pepper to taste
1 tsp cornstarch
12 sheets of filo dough

Fry ground meat in butter until meat has stopped giving off juice and half the moisture has evaporated. Add minced onion and green pepper. Cook 10 minutes more or until onion and pepper are soft. Remove from fire and mix in herbs, pine nuts, and seasoning; the mixture should be somewhat peppery. Cool and chill well. Just before making the beoregs, sprinkle cornstarch over meat mixture. The starch will absorb excess moisture that may accumulate while the beoreg bakes.

Roll filling in filo dough as described on pages 31–33. Bake them in a preheated 300° oven 20–30 minutes or until golden brown. Serve very hot.

CHEESE BEOREGS

SERVINGS: 10–12 regular beoregs, or 4 doz. cocktail beoregs

1 lb. Munster (or any soft yellow cheese)
¼ lb. feta cheese
¾ lb. pot cheese
1 egg
¼ cup minced parsley
2 Tb minced dill
12 sheets of filo dough

Grate Munster and feta cheese. Mix with all other ingredients. Because feta cheese is usually very salty, additional salt will probably not be needed. Roll and bake as in preceding recipe.

CHICK-PEA PASTE

SERVINGS: ⅔ cup

> ½ cup chick-peas, dried or canned
> tip of 1 garlic clove
> 4 tsp sesame seed paste (sesame tahini)
> ½ tsp salt
> 1 Tb water
> 1 Tb lemon juice
> 2 Tb olive oil

Cook chick-peas until they are extremely soft. (Uncooked, dried chick-peas should be soaked overnight and simmered slowly for 2 hours or more.)

Crush tip of garlic clove in a mortar, add cooked, drained chick-peas, mash them, and gradually mix in all remaining ingredients.

Serve with Armenian Bread (page 185) during a meal or with assorted appetizers as a first course.

EGGPLANT CAVIAR

Usually used as a spread or dip with crackers, Caucasian and Middle Asian flat breads, and melba toast, eggplant caviar is made in many different ways. Two versions are given below.

EGGPLANT CAVIAR (I)

SERVINGS: 6 (with other appetizers)

1 small, young eggplant
2 Tb sesame seed paste (tahini)
2 tsp lemon juice
½ garlic clove, pressed
1–2 Tb olive oil
salt to taste

Bake eggplant in a low oven until it is thoroughly soft. Remove pulp and mash it. Mix in the sesame seed paste, lemon juice, and pressed or crushed garlic clove. Add olive oil slowly in a thin stream while mixing. Season with salt and serve chilled.

EGGPLANT CAVIAR (II)

SERVINGS: 6 (with other appetizers)

1 medium eggplant (about 3 cups when cubed)
1 tsp salt
2 Tb plus 2 tsp olive oil
¾ cup minced onion
salt and ground pepper to taste
lemon juice to taste
½ clove garlic (optional)

Peel and cube eggplant, discarding seeds. Sprinkle with 1 tsp salt and let it stand 1 hour. Squeeze eggplant to eliminate liquid. Heat 2 Tb olive oil in a frying pan or casserole. Fry eggplant slowly with minced onion until both are very soft. Chop them with the edge of a spatula while frying. Off fire, stir in 2 tsp olive oil, salt and pepper and lemon juice to taste. If you like garlic, press or crush ½ clove and add. Chill before serving.

ROSSOLYE

Estonian Mixed Salad

This cold salad is particularly good with vodka as an appetizer or first course. Sometimes it is served with cold sliced meat on the side. It makes an excellent winter buffet dish and appears at every Estonian party. It is also a must in Lithuanian gatherings, where it is known as vinegretas and contains more vegetables—peas, dried white beans, cauliflower, and more carrot.

SERVINGS: 6

SALAD

2 thick slices of cold meat, cubed*
1 cooked carrot, cubed*
1 small raw onion, diced
2–3 firm, boiled potatoes, peeled and cubed*
1 raw apple, cored, peeled, and cubed*
½ herring, cubed*
1 sour dill pickle, cubed*
3 beets, cooked and peeled (or canned)
2 hard-boiled eggs

DRESSING

1 cup sour cream
2 Tb sharp mustard
2 Tb vinegar
1 tsp sugar
salt to taste

---

* ½" cubes.

Combine the first 5 salad ingredients in a bowl and mix the dressing separately. Keep both in a cool place until ready to serve. Just before serving, mix herring and pickle into salad, toss it in dressing, and decorate it with slices of beet and hard-boiled egg.

SALADE OLIVIER

Russians named this salad after Tsar Nicolas II's chef, who created it. Outside Russia, it is more often called Salade Russe and is sometimes reduced to a simple mixture of cooked vegetables in mayonnaise that bears little resemblance to the original.

SERVINGS: 8

3 medium-size, firm potatoes
2–3 young carrots, or 1 package frozen carrots (optional)
3 young beetroots, or 1 small can sliced beets
2 chicken breasts (breasts of 1 chicken)
4 eggs
½ bunch spring onions
½ cucumber
1 thick slice cooked ham

DRESSING

1 cup mayonnaise
½ cup sour cream
2 dill pickles (without garlic), diced
2 Tb tomato paste (optional)
1 Tb prepared mustard
1 Tb capers
2 Tb minced dill and parsley
salt and pepper to taste

Boil, peel, and dice potatoes; discard soft and irregular parts. Boil and cube carrots and beetroots separately, reserving 1 beet for decoration. Poach chicken breasts 5–6 minutes or until cooked through, and cube when cooled. Hard-boil the eggs and chop 2 of them. Cut the cleaned spring onions in rounds; use the tender green part too. Peel and cube cucumber. Cube the ham. Mix ingredients only after they have all reached room temperature, and keep beets apart until just before serving. Take care not to bruise the tender vegetables. Cover bowl and place in refrigerator to chill.

Combine ingredients for dressing, but do not mix with salad until ready to serve. Decorate salad with slices of remaining hard-boiled eggs and sliced beet.

ARMENIAN WHITE BEAN SALAD

SERVINGS: 6 (with other appetizers)

1 cup dried pea beans, soaked in water overnight
4 Tb olive oil
4 Tb lemon juice
1 tsp ground coriander
salt and ground white pepper to taste
1 heaping Tb minced parsley

Drain soaked beans, put them over a low fire with enough water to rise 1″ above the beans, and cook slowly until tender. Add small amounts of water as needed. When beans are cooked (2–3 hours), there should be almost no liquid left. Toss hot beans in olive oil and lemon juice with coriander, salt, and pepper. Chill. Mix in freshly minced parsley before serving.

LOBIO

Kidney Beans in Walnut Sauce

In Georgia, cold kidney beans are often served as one of several dishes composing a first course.

SERVINGS: 6

> 1½ cups dry kidney beans
> salt to taste
> ¼ cup shelled walnuts
> ½ clove garlic
> 1 small piece fresh or dried chili pepper, or cayenne
>   pepper to taste
> 2 Tb wine vinegar
> ⅓ cup water
> 1 small onion, minced
> 1 Tb minced parsley
> 1 Tb minced fresh coriander, or ¼ tsp ground
>   coriander

Sort over and wash beans. Unless they are the quick-cooking variety, soak them in water several hours in advance. To cook, cover them with fresh water in a casserole and simmer slowly until soft, adding small amounts of boiling water as needed. When beans are soft, pour off cooking water and salt beans to taste.

Pound walnuts to a paste with garlic clove and red pepper. Blend in vinegar and water. Taking care not to bruise the beans, mix in walnut paste, minced onion, and herbs. Chill before serving.

LOBIO WITH POMEGRANATE JUICE AND WALNUTS

Prepare kidney beans as in the preceding recipe, but substitute ¼ cup pomegranate juice and ¼ cup water

for the wine vinegar and water. Sprinkle chilled salad
with seeds from a fresh pomegranate.

RADISHES IN SOUR CREAM

About the closest thing to a salad in the heart of
Russia, this dish is usually served as one of many
appetizers.

SERVINGS: 1 small bowlful or enough for 4–6 if served
with other dishes

> *1 bunch radishes*
> *½ tsp salt*
> *3 Tb sour cream*
> *1 tsp vinegar*
> *a sprinkling of black pepper*

Rinse and dry radishes. Slice thin, but not paper-thin.
Place in shallow dish and sprinkle with salt. After ½
hour, drain off excess water. Stir in sour cream, vinegar,
and pepper. Serve chilled.

ESTONIAN CUCUMBER SALAD

SERVINGS: 4–6

> *2 cucumbers*
> *salt*
> *4 Tb sour cream*
> *2 Tb lemon juice*
> *½ tsp sugar*
> *⅛ tsp salt for dressing*

Peel cucumbers and slice paper-thin. Arrange in layers in a dish, sprinkling each layer lightly with salt. Let cucumbers remain in salt 2–3 hours, then squeeze them thoroughly to extract juice. Mix sour cream, lemon juice, sugar, and ⅛ tsp salt in a bowl. Stir in cucumbers. Serve chilled.

NOTE: Estonians sometimes serve sliced, salted, and squeezed cucumbers with nothing more than a sprinkling of caraway seed.

QUICK BELORUSSIAN CUCUMBER PICKLES

SERVINGS: 4–6 as a relish

These are pickles to be made in the morning and eaten at night. They can be kept for the following day, but will lose the crispness that is part of their charm. It is therefore best to make no more than needed at one time. The brine can be saved, sharpened with a bit of vinegar and sugar, and used for 2 or more batches.

5–6 cucumbers
½ medium onion
1 small garlic clove, crushed
1 Tb fresh dill, chopped, or 2 tsp dried dill
2 cups of water
6 Tb wine vinegar
4 Tb sugar
1 Tb salt

Peel cucumbers, cut them lengthwise in slices about ⅜″ thick, and spread them in 2 or 3 layers in a shallow container. Slice onion on top of cover, spread crushed garlic over the surface, and sprinkle with dill.

Mix water, vinegar, sugar, and salt and pour it over

cucumber slices. If you like pickles very crisp, do not heat the liquid. If you like them limper, yellower, and more like commercial pickles, bring the liquid to a boil before pouring it over. Mix additional brine in the same proportions if needed to cover the cucumbers.

The pickles will be ready to eat in about 6 hours.

QUICK SWEET PEPPER PICKLES

The brine for Belorussian cucumber pickles can be used to pickle sweet green peppers. Remove tops and seeds, wash and dry peppers, cut them in large pieces, and cover with brine, onions, and garlic as in the preceding recipe. A single portion of brine will cover 6 or more small peppers.

CHAPTER THREE

SOUPS

Soups play an important role in Russian meals and are often an entire meal by themselves. Russian shchi and Ukrainian borshch in their diverse forms are the two staple soups of the north. Barley and other grain soups are popular in Lithuania and the Ukraine. Fish soups are made wherever fish is locally available, and there is a wide range of refreshing cold soups for the hot summer: fruit soups from the north, yogurt soups flavored with dried mint from the Caucasus, and sour milk soups from Central Asia. The Caucasus and Central Asia have substantial soups as well—soups with chunks of lamb, dried vegetables, potatoes and other starches, fresh vegetables, herbs, and sometimes even fruit and nuts, all cooked in little liquid.

BORSHCH

Borshch originated in the Ukraine, where it is the national soup. It is a bouillon made tart by the addition of lemon juice, vinegar, or, in the old-fashioned way, by a fermented liquid made of rye or beets and known as kvass. It also always contains root vegetables, principally beets; the name "borshch" comes from an old Slavic

word for beet. Although there are one or two soups
without beets that go by that name, the statement
that borshch is a beet soup will hardly ever be
contradicted.

Like most good peasant dishes, borshch made its way
to the capital and to neighboring countries, where new
versions were invented. There are as many borshchs as
there are cooks, but those from the same region share
specific characteristics. In general, the farther west you
go in the U.S.S.R., the more beets you find in the borshch,
with the largest portion in the Western Ukraine. There,
in fact, beets are the only vegetable in the soup, which
is often known as borshchok. Central Ukrainians like a
large amount of cabbage; Muscovites reduce the number
of beets until borshch becomes more of a vegetable soup.
Northern Russians use beef almost exclusively, Ukrainians
often use pork, and Belorussians like to put in three kinds
of meat.

In the Ukraine, each version of borshch is named after
the region in which it is made. One thing all versions
have in common is a large number of ingredients: 15–20
on an average. Ukrainian Borshch almost always contains
some fat in the form of bacon, which is chopped or
crushed with garlic, onions, herbs, or carrots, and added
to the soup toward the end of its cooking. Old-style
borshch starts with a bouillon of meat and chopped
bones, and the fat from the soup is used to sauté the
vegetables. Each area has its individual list of ingredients.
For example, Poltava borshch is made with chicken or
goose and served with buckwheat dumplings; Chernihiv
borshch has squash, sour apples, and white beans, and
Lvov borshch is garnished with cooked, sliced sausages.

A good borshch must overcome two problems: (1)
keeping the meat and vegetables flavorful as well as the
stock, and (2) preserving the rich red color of the beets.
The first is generally solved by cooking the meat separately and removing it, and then cooking the vegetables
in the broth in a specific order that gives each just time
to become tender. To keep their color, beets are usually

cooked apart from the stock, sometimes—particularly in the Ukraine—in vinegar or beet kvass.

Borshch is always better the second day. I make it the day before serving it to guests and find each time that it has improved immeasurably overnight. Sometimes, to my disappointment, I find it has reached its peak only on the third day, when the guests are gone.

Borshch can be hot or cold; the cold version is served without meat and sometimes made without it. In the latter case, it is often called a hlodnik (or kholodnik), a general term for cold soups in Poland, the Ukraine, and Lithuania. Canned consommé or beef bouillon can be substituted for meat stock in the following recipes or used to strengthen a meat stock made with less meat than called for in the recipe. However, there is more than one advantage in cooking a large piece of meat in the soup. Not only does it give the bouillon a richer flavor, it also provides you with quantities of boiled meat. There is nothing better than cold boiled meat with a little sour-cream horseradish sauce and a salad as a cold supper (page 147). Furthermore, boiled meat is an essential part of the fillings of almost all of the delicious soup accompaniments: pirozhky, pelmeny, lietiniai, nalysnyky, and others (see Chapter Four). And served in the soup or on the side, meat makes borshch a hearty meal.

UKRAINIAN BORSHCH (I)

Ukrainians like a hearty borshch with some pork or pork fat in it and a great variety of vegetables. This borshch is a meal in itself.

SERVINGS: 8–10

4–6 lbs. pork, beef, or a combination of both
14 cups cold water
6 peppercorns
1 large bay leaf
salt to taste
5–6 raw beets
2 potatoes, cut in large cubes
2–3 carrots, cut in strips
1 cup chopped canned or fresh tomatoes
½ large onion, chopped
½ small head cabbage, shredded
½ cup cooked or canned white beans
2 Tb flour
2–3 Tb lemon juice
1 or more tsp sugar (to taste)
a piece of smoked salt pork the size of an egg
1 tsp minced parsley
1 small piece raw onion, or 1 clove peeled garlic
a bowl of sour cream

Cover meat with water, bring to a boil with peppercorns and bay leaf, skim twice, cover, and simmer until meat is tender. Skim off grease,* salt to taste.

An hour before serving, add beets, potatoes, carrots, tomatoes, and onion. Add cabbage and beans ½ hour later. Correct seasoning. Blend 2 Tb flour with a little cold water; stir in a bit of liquid from soup, and add to soup. Just before serving, mix in lemon juice and sugar to taste. Mash salt pork in a mortar or bowl with minced parsley and raw onion or garlic. Stir mixture into soup. Serve with sour cream on the side.

---

* The grease is easiest to remove if the meat is cooked far enough in advance so that the stock can be allowed to cool, and the grease to congeal.

UKRAINIAN BORSHCH (II)

This second Ukrainian borshch is meant to be served without meat as a first course, accompanied by pirozhky made from the meat (page 90).

SERVINGS: 15–18

>   3 lbs. beef for soup (chuck, brisket, etc.)
>   3 qts. cold water
>   1 medium onion, coarsely chopped
>   1 bay leaf
>   1 parsley root
>   2 tsp salt
>   3 medium-size raw beets
>   ½ cup tomato sauce
>   1 Tb wine vinegar
>   2 large carrots, sliced
>   4 medium potatoes
>   1 small head cabbage, shredded
>   3 slices of bacon
>   1 large onion
>   salt and pepper to taste
>   a bowl of sour cream

Cover meat with cold water. Add onion, bay leaf, cleaned parsley root, and salt. Bring to a boil, reduce heat, and simmer until meat is tender (2 hours or more). Remove meat, skim off grease and strain soup stock, and reheat.

Peel beets and cut them into shoestring strips. Cook them, covered, over low fire with tomato sauce, 1 Tb vinegar, and ½ cup bouillon from the soup. Add 2 large, sliced carrots to soup. Cook 10 minutes more. Add potatoes, peeled and cut in large chunks. Add shredded cabbage. When vegetables and beets are tender, add beets and the sauce in which they were cooked to the soup.

Dice 3 slices of bacon and chop 1 large onion. Fry them together until bacon is crisp. Strain off fat and add mixture to soup. Season to taste with salt and pepper. Let soup boil once and set it aside for 15–20 minutes. Serve it with a bowl of sour cream on the side.

SIMPLE RUSSIAN BORSHCH

The following recipe contains the essential elements of borshch with no strong regional characteristics.

SERVINGS: 8–10

> 4–6 lbs. soup beef*
> 14 cups of cold water
> 6 peppercorns
> 1 large bay leaf
> 5–6 raw beets
> ½ small head cabbage
> salt to taste
> 2–3 Tb lemon juice
> 1 or more tsp sugar to taste
> a bowl of sour cream
> minced dill (optional)

Remove some of the thick fat from the meat, but not all of it. Put the meat in a large casserole with 14 cups cold water, 6 peppercorns and 1 bay leaf. Bring it to a boil, skim it twice, cover it, leaving a small opening for the escape of steam, and cook it at a low boil 2–3 hours or until meat is tender. Remove meat. Strain stock and remove grease.

About an hour before serving, wash the raw beets, remove their tops without nicking the beetroot, and cook

---

* Use 4 lbs. if meat is to be served in the soup; 6 if it is to be a separate course.

the roots in boiling salt water until tender (20–30 minutes for young beets; more for large, old ones). Next, wash and shred cabbage and add it to meat broth. Add salt to taste. When beets are cooked, peel them, cut them in long strips (julienne), add them to soup, and let soup boil twice. Stir in 2–3 Tb lemon juice to give soup a tart (but not sour) taste. If the beets are not sweet, add 1 tsp or more sugar. The borshch is now ready to serve with the meat on the side, as a second course, or cut in cubes and reheated in the soup. If meat is not served with the soup, some side dish should be offered (see Chapter Four).

Sour cream is always served with borshch. Some cooks stir it into the slightly cooled soup before serving, but this spoils the next day's leftovers. It is more prudent to serve the sour cream in a bowl on the side. Mix in a little minced fresh dill, if you choose.

BELORUSSIAN BORSHCH

SERVINGS: 8–10

1½ lbs. pork shoulder
1½ lbs. chuck
1½ lbs. lamb shank or neck bones
14 cups of cold water
6 peppercorns
1 large bay leaf
5–6 raw beets
½ small head cabbage
salt to taste
2 carrots, cut in strips
1 small onion or a few spring onions, chopped
1 cup canned or fresh tomatoes, chopped
2 Tb lemon juice
1 or more tsp sugar
a bowl of sour cream

Cook first 8 ingredients as described in Simple Russian
Borshch (page 50). Add all other vegetables 1 hour
before soup is to be served. Stir in lemon juice and sugar
for desired balance of sweet and sour taste. Serve with
a bowl of sour cream on the side.

BORSHCHOK

Borshchok is served hot and is made with meat, but
beets are the only vegetable. It is very popular in the
Western Ukraine, where beets dominate the vegetable
crop.

SERVINGS: 8

>*2 bunches of young beets*
>*2 sliced onions*
>*2 lbs. plate brisket*
>*8 cups water*
>*juice of 2 lemons*
>*2 Tb sugar (use more or less according to taste)*
>*2 tsp salt*
>*pepper to taste*
>*croutons (bread, fried or toasted in cubes until crisp)*

Peel and dice beets. Place beets, onions, and meat in
deep pot. Add water and bring to a boil. Reduce flame
and simmer until meat is tender. Cube meat and return
it to pot. Add lemon juice, sugar, salt, and pepper.
Simmer 10 minutes longer. Serve hot with a garnish of
crumbled croutons.

BELORUSSIAN COLD BORSHCH

SERVINGS: 8

2 bunches young beets with beet greens
2 cups cold water
1 large onion, chopped fairly fine
2 cups hot meat stock or bouillon
2½ cups tomato juice
salt and pepper to taste
1 small cucumber, peeled and chopped
½ bunch spring onions, chopped
2 hard-boiled eggs, chopped
1–2 Tb sour cream per person

Wash beets and remove tops without cutting into beet-root. Put beets in boiling water, cover, and cook until tender. While beets cook, put 2 cups cold water on fire in large pot with 1 large, chopped onion. Cover pot and cook gently while washing and chopping beet leaves. Blanch leaves by dropping them in boiling water for 1 minute, then rinsing them in a sieve under cold water. Set them aside.

When beetroots are cooked, drain them, discard the cooking water, and peel and cut them in long thin strips (julienne). As soon as the onions are thoroughly cooked, add them to the blanched beet greens. Stir in the beets, the hot stock or bouillon, and the tomato juice. Mix well. Season soup to taste with salt and pepper, remove it from fire, and let it cool. After chilling it in the refrigerator, serve it with chopped cucumber, chopped fresh spring onion, chopped hard-boiled eggs, and sour cream, all either on the side or placed in the individual bowls.

NOTE: Although this soup is meant to be eaten cold, it is also good hot. When serving hot, omit cucumbers, spring onions, and hard-boiled eggs.

ŽALBARŠČIAI
Cold Lithuanian Borshch

Pronounced *zhal'-barsh-chay* in Lithuanian, this is a
very quickly made and refreshing soup. If you can get
young beet tops, try the early spring version Lithuanians
make before the vegetable roots are mature: substitute
beet tops and the juice in which they cooked for the
beets in the following recipe.

SERVINGS: 4

> 1 1-lb. can of small whole beets, or 1 bunch of fresh
>   beets, peeled and boiled until tender
> juice from canned beets, or 1 cup of the water in
>   which fresh beets were cooked
> 3 cups buttermilk
> 1 heaping Tb sour cream
> 2 hard-boiled eggs, chopped
> ½ fresh cucumber, peeled and diced
> ⅛ tsp sugar
> 4 Tb minced spring onion tops
> 2 Tb minced fresh dill (if available)
> bowl of sour cream (optional)

Grate beets and mix with juice from can or 1 cup of
water from the cooking of fresh beets. Chill thoroughly.
When beet juice is very cold, mix in buttermilk, sour
cream, chopped hard-boiled eggs, diced cucumber, and
sugar. Sprinkle with minced onion tops and dill. Additional sour cream may be served in a bowl on the side.

STORING AND REVIVING BORSHCH

The meat from borshch is best left in the bouillon to
cool, if time permits. This keeps it from forming a crust,
but is of importance only when the meat is to be served
cold. Reheated, it becomes soft again.

While meat should be kept in the refrigerator, soup can be kept several days at room temperature providing it is brought to a rolling boil once a day in winter and twice in summer.

Beets cooked too long or reheated too often take on a brown color, unattractive in borshch. To give brownish borshch a good red color, grate a fresh raw beet into it and simmer the soup 10 minutes. Another way to restore color is to add a beet infusion: grate 1 or 2 fresh beets, simmer them in a little hot bouillon with 1 tsp lemon juice or vinegar for 15 minutes, and strain the liquid over the soup.

SHCHI

Green Vegetable Soup

> *Shchi da kasha,*
> *Nasha pishcha.*

"Shchi and kasha, that's our food" goes the old Russian couplet. Shchi is the most popular Russian soup. It is a meat bouillon in which cabbage predominates. If the cabbage is fresh, the soup is called simply shchi; if it is in the form of sauerkraut, the soup is called sour shchi. In many areas, fresh cabbage and sauerkraut are combined, and this is the version of sour shchi included here. Other root vegetables, sometimes first sautéed in butter, are added to shchi, and the soup is thickened with flour or diced potatoes. Sour cream is mixed into the soup as well as being served on the side, and it is traditional to serve shchi with some of the meat from the stock cut up in it.

There are three other related shchis. The one made of the very first cabbage sprouts is a country specialty. It is easy to imagine how eagerly the peasants pounce on the first green sprouts pushing through the thick clods of thawing earth after eating only sauerkraut soup all winter. Another seasonal soup, a later spring dish, is known as green shchi. This is a spinach and sorrel soup that can be made only when the sorrel that grows wild through parts of Russia is ripe.* The third is a shchi made with nettles, picked before they are grown enough to sting.

SHCHI
Russian Cabbage Soup

SERVINGS: 6–8

> 3–4 lbs. soup beef (chuck, lean short ribs, brisket, shank)
> 12 cups water
> 6 peppercorns
> 1 large bay leaf
> 2 carrots, cleaned and sliced
> 1 small cabbage, shredded
> salt to taste
> 1 cup sour cream
> 1 large onion, or 2 bunches spring onions, chopped
> 2 Tb butter or fat from meat bouillon†
> 2 Tb flour
> 3 Tb minced parsley or dill or a combination of both

Put meat in a large pot with water, peppercorns, and bay leaf. Bring to a rapid boil, skim twice, then reduce heat, cover, and simmer for 2 hours or until meat is tender. Remove meat and put it aside. Strain soup and skim grease from surface.

About 1 hour before serving, fry carrots and onion gently in butter or fat. When onions are transparent and

---

* Not to be confused with shchav, which is plain sorrel soup (shchavel means sorrel in Russian).

† Save 2 Tb of the pure fat obtained in skimming the soup.

golden, sprinkle flour over them. Gradually stir in boiling broth. Add shredded cabbage, cover, and simmer 30 minutes. Season to taste with salt.

Add meat, cut in bite-size pieces, 10 minutes before the soup is to be served. If the soup is not a main course, put in only half the meat or less and save the remainder for another meal. Let the soup cool a little before stirring in ½ cup sour cream. Sprinkle soup with minced fresh herbs and serve with remaining cream in a bowl on the side.

VARIATIONS ON FRESH CABBAGE SHCHI

A number of vegetables can be added to those in the basic recipe for shchi. For example:

1–2 turnips, peeled and cut in strips 2"–3" long
1 parsnip, sliced
1 stalk celery, chopped
2 large fresh tomatoes, peeled and chopped, or 1 medium can
3 potatoes, cut in large pieces

Brown turnips, parsnip, and celery lightly with the carrots and onions. Add tomatoes and potatoes along with cabbage 30 minutes before serving time.

SOUR SHCHI
(Sauerkraut Soup)

This is a Belorussian version of the famous soup. Unlike Russian versions, it combines three kinds of meat as Belorussians, Ukrainians, and Lithuanians love to do. The recipe comes from a Belorussian grandmother who, even transplanted to Chicago, used to prepare her own wooden barrel of cabbage and salt in the summer for the winter's sour shchi.

SERVINGS: 8

> 1½ lbs. pork shoulder or butt
> 1 lb. lamb shank or neck bones
> 2 lbs. beef chuck
> 12 cups water
> 6–8 peppercorns
> 1 bay leaf
> 1 onion
> ½ small head cabbage (½ lb.)
> 1½ cups sauerkraut, drained (1-lb. package or can)
> 2 small potatoes, peeled and diced
> 1 carrot, grated
> 2 Tb tomato paste, or 1 8-oz. can of tomatoes
> 1 tsp caraway seed (if sauerkraut does not contain it)
> salt to taste
> a bowl of sour cream

Put all 3 meats in a large pot. Add water, peppercorns, bay leaf, and onion. Bring to a boil. Skim twice, reduce flame, adjust lid so that pot is almost entirely covered, and leave on low boil until meat is nearly done (2–2½ hours).

Remove meat, skim off grease, and strain soup through a sieve lined with several layers of cheesecloth. Return soup and meat to pot.

Shred ½ small head cabbage. Blanch by immersing in boiling water for 1 minute, then rinsing in cold. Drain sauerkraut, reserving liquid. Add cabbage and sauerkraut to soup with 2 diced potatoes, 1 grated carrot, the tomato paste or tomatoes, and 1 tsp caraway seed. Simmer soup another ½ hour or more.

Before serving, taste soup and add a little of the reserved sauerkraut juice if the soup is not tart. Season with salt only after adding the sauerkraut and juice because canned sauerkraut is sometimes quite salty. Remove meat, cut up a portion in bite-size pieces, and

reheat them in soup. If the soup is to be the main part
of the meal, cut up 1 slice of meat per serving, but if it
is a first course, use only ½ slice or less.

Serve soup in large bowls with a dish of sour cream on
the side.

GREEN SHCHI
(Sorrel-and-Spinach Soup)

SERVINGS: 8

> *1 lb. fresh young sorrel leaves*
> *1½ Tb butter*
> *1 lb. raw spinach*
> *a pinch of salt*
> *1 Tb flour*
> *3 qts. beef bouillon, or stock made according to recipe*
>   *for shchi on page 56 with 3 lbs. soup beef, pepper-*
>   *corns, and bay leaf*
> *½ cup sour cream or sour milk*

Wash sorrel leaves, squeeze out water, and chop them.
Put them in a casserole with juice given off while
chopping. Simmer over low heat with ½ Tb butter until
tender, then force through strainer.

Wash spinach, add salt and a little water, and cook
spinach, uncovered, until done. Rinse under cold water
in strainer. Drain well. Force through strainer and add
to sorrel.

Melt 1 Tb butter in a large pot. Mix in 1 Tb flour and
cook for 1 minute while stirring. Gradually add stock or
bouillon. Stir in vegetables, bring to a boil, and remove
from heat. Cool soup slightly before adding sour cream.

Serve sprinkled with chopped hard-boiled egg or with
a side dish of Hard-Boiled Eggs, Hot Stuffed Eggs, or
Kasha Squares (pages 75, 75, 76).

SIBERIAN OUHA

Ouha (or oukha) is traditionally a clear fish soup. This is a clear soup, but made with ham instead of fish. Nevertheless, the Russian restaurant that gave me the recipe (Sasha's, of Chicago) calls it Siberian Ouha, and, in any case, it is delicious.

SERVINGS: 6–8

>   1 ham bone (or packaged ham base)
>   8 cups cold water
>   2 slices ham
>   ½ clove garlic, peeled and left whole
>   ½ small head cabbage, chopped fine
>   1¼ cups canned tomatoes
>   1 bunch spring onions
>   a generous quantity of dill, minced
>   salt to taste, and an equal amount of sugar

Cover ham bone with 8 cups cold water and put it to simmer. Cut ham in julienne strips (thin slivers about 2″ long) and add them to soup. Add garlic, chopped cabbage, tomatoes with juice, chopped stalks of spring onion, and minced dill. Simmer approximately 1½ hours or until cabbage is cooked and ham bone has given sufficient flavor to soup. Salt only when soup is almost ready and with caution: the ham may be quite salty. Measure the amount of salt and add an equal amount of sugar.

NOTE: If made with ham base instead of a ham bone, the soup can be prepared very quickly by starting with hot water instead of cold. The soup is done as soon as the ham strips and cabbage are tender.

CHIKHIRTMA

Chikhirtma is a popular soup in the Caucasus and Central Asia. Usually made with chicken, it can also be made with lamb. It is always thickened with egg yolks for richness and usually given a tart flavor with lemon or vinegar. The degree of tartness and richness can be varied in the following recipes to suit individual preferences. In some regions, the soup is made more substantial by the cooking of a few cubed carrots and potatoes in the broth prior to the addition of egg yolks.

CHICKEN CHIKHIRTMA

SERVINGS: 6

6 cups chicken stock* or canned chicken broth
1½ cups finely chopped onion
1 Tb butter
1 Tb flour
a pinch of saffron, dissolved in ¼ cup hot water (optional)
salt to taste
3 egg yolks
3 Tb lemon juice
several Tb minced fresh herbs (parsley, coriander, dill, basil, tarragon)

Heat stock while frying onion until golden in butter. Sprinkle flour over onion and stir over fire for 1 minute. Spoon a little broth into mixture, blend well, and pour mixture into pot containing broth. Cook 10 minutes. If

* If using homemade stock, reheat some small pieces of the chicken in the soup before serving.

using saffron, dissolve it in hot water and strain the liquid into broth. Salt to taste. Remove from fire.

Beat egg yolks with lemon juice. Mix a little broth into this liquid, then pour the mixture into the pot of broth while stirring. Reheat broth until it thickens, stirring constantly and not allowing it to come to a boil. Serve sprinkled with chopped fresh herbs.

LAMB CHIKHIRTMA

SERVINGS: 6–8

¾ lb. lamb, cut in small pieces
6 cups water
1 cup chopped onion
1 Tb butter
1 Tb flour
salt to taste
2 Tb vinegar
6 egg yolks
several Tb minced fresh herbs (parsley, coriander, dill, basil)

Cover meat with cold water. Put on lid and cook over low fire until meat is very tender and has given flavor to water (1–1½ hours). When stock is done, fry onion gently in butter until golden. Sprinkle flour over onion and continue to cook while stirring for 1 minute. Mix in a few spoonfuls of the stock and blend thoroughly. Stir mixture into pot of broth and cook 10 minutes more. Salt soup to taste. Add vinegar and let soup boil once. Then remove it from fire.

Beat egg yolks in a separate bowl. Stir a little soup into yolks; pour mixture into broth while stirring. Continue to stir while reheating soup without permitting it to boil. Serve sprinkled with minced fresh herbs.

BOZBASH

Azerbaidzhani Mutton-and-Vegetable Soup

This a thick, substantial soup as Azerbaidzhani soups generally are.

SERVINGS: 6

1 lb. lamb or mutton, cut in large serving pieces
8 cups water
6 Tb dried split peas
2 medium potatoes
2 medium onions
4 Tb tomato paste
salt and pepper to taste
a scant tsp of crushed dried mint

Wash meat in cold water. Put it in a casserole with 8 cups cold water and split peas (previously soaked if required by directions on package). Cook 1½–2 hours or until meat and peas are tender. Cube potatoes, chop onions, and add them with tomato paste about 20 minutes before meat and split peas are ready. Season with salt and pepper to taste. Pour into individual bowls and serve sprinkled with dried mint, crushed to a powder.

SOLIANKA

Russian Fish Soup

Solianka is traditionally made with sturgeon, but any firm white fish will do. It makes a hearty first course, or, with a large portion of fish in it, a lunch or light supper. It can be kept for several days in the refrigerator if stored in tightly closed jars.

The following recipe is for making Solianka alone, but it is easy to combine with the preparation of fish in aspic (see page 114).

SERVINGS: 6

> 1 fish head
> 6 cups water (more if necessary to cover ingredients)
> 1 Tb salt
> 6 peppercorns
> 1 bay leaf
> soup greens (1 celery top, 1 leek, 1 turnip or parsnip
>   or both, 1 carrot, several sprigs parsley and dill)
> 2 lbs. sturgeon, swordfish, or other firm white fish
> 4 Tb capers
> 10 black olives preserved in olive oil
> 4 Tb tomato paste
> 2 Tb olive oil
> salt to taste
> ¼–½ tsp sugar
> ¼–½ tsp baking soda if needed

Wash fish head, wrap in cheesecloth, and put in water with salt, peppercorns, bay leaf, and cleaned soup greens. Simmer slowly ¾–1 hour. Wrap cleaned fish in cheesecloth and soak it in cold water 5 minutes. Add fish to soup and cook 10–20 minutes, or until fish is done.

Remove fish and fish head. Bone fish and cut it in bite-size pieces; put them aside. (Remove meat from fish head too.) Strain soup through fine sieve lined with 3 layers of cheesecloth. Mash vegetables in a mortar, colander, or blender. Return soup to fire with mashed vegetables. Wrap fish head and bones carefully in cheesecloth and return them to soup also. Add capers, olives (pitted and cut in half), tomato paste, and olive oil. Stir well, add salt to taste and ¼–½ tsp sugar. If soup is sour rather than tart, add a tiny bit more sugar or a little baking soda (¼–½ tsp). Simmer soup another

45 minutes. Before serving, remove cheesecloth containing fish head and bones, and reheat in the soup the pieces of fish meat set aside earlier.

TARGHANA SOUP

Armenian Yogurt Soup

Targhana Soup can be made with commercially prepared targhana (or trahana), available in Middle Eastern and Armenian groceries. It is a distinctive and quickly made soup which anyone fond of yogurt will find superb. A recipe for preparing the Targhana at home is given on page 66.

At the excellent Armenian restaurant in New York, the Dardanelles (which contributed this recipe), the soup is served with Armenian Bread (page 185), oven-toasted with a little butter. According to the chef of the Dardanelles, old-time Armenians liked the bread fried in grease and the onion in the soup deliberately burned instead of lightly browned. The change in tastes, in this case, seems to have been for the better.

SERVINGS: 10–12

    ½ cup dry Targhana
    2½ qts. meat broth (stock or canned beef bouillon or
        consommé)
    1½ cups minced onion
    4 Tb butter
    1 Tb crushed dried mint
    1½ cups yogurt

An hour before starting the soup, put the Targhana to soak. When it has soaked 1 hour, bring the meat broth to a boil, add Targhana mixture, and cook, stirring occasionally, for 15 minutes. While broth cooks, fry minced onion slowly in butter until golden brown. Add crushed mint and cook 10 seconds more. Stir onion and mint into meat broth and simmer 5 minutes longer. Let broth cool slightly before adding yogurt, then serve at once.

NOTE: Targhana Soup can be prepared in advance to the point of adding yogurt and completed at the last moment.

HOMEMADE TARGHANA FOR SOUP

SERVINGS: Enough for 5–6 recipes of Targhana Soup

⅓ oz. yeast
1 cup warm water
½ lb. all-purpose flour, sifted
½ tsp salt
½ lb. cracked wheat No. 3
1 cup yogurt

Dissolve yeast in a little of the warm water, then mix in remaining water. Sift flour with salt and add it to yeast with remaining ingredients. Knead until well blended. Leave covered with a cloth overnight.

The following day, divide dough into 6 pieces. Roll each out about ⅛″ thick. Leave pieces in a dry place on a cloth until the following day; turn them over and leave them again until thoroughly dried. Break dried dough into small bits and store it in tightly closed jars for use as needed.

NOTE: The drying process can be speeded by putting the rolled dough in a warm oven.

AZERBAIDZHANI LENTIL SOUP

SERVINGS: 4

1 cup lentils
6 cups water
1 potato
1 tomato
1 onion
2 Tb butter
salt and pepper to taste

Bring lentils and water to a boil slowly in a saucepan or casserole. Skim foam from top, cover, and let cook slowly 1–2 hours, or until lentils are quite soft. Add peeled, sliced potato and continue cooking 1 hour. Fry peeled, chopped tomato with minced onion in butter until onion is tender. Add this to soup and cook 15 minutes longer. Season with salt and pepper. Continue cooking 4–5 minutes and serve.

KRUPENIK

Barley-and-Mushroom Soup

SERVINGS: 4–6

1½ oz. dried mushrooms
2 cups water
½ cup barley
8 cups beef stock, bouillon, or consommé
salt to taste
6 Tb sour cream at room temperature

Wash mushrooms, rinse, and soak in 2 cups water several hours overnight before starting soup. Save water.

Strain water in which mushrooms soaked through cheesecloth. Combine water with rinsed barley, chopped mushrooms, and stock. Bring to a boil and simmer, tightly covered, until barley and mushrooms are entirely soft (1 hour or more). Salt to taste. Cool soup slightly before stirring in sour cream.

OKROSHKA

Okroshka is something like Spanish gazpacho: you hardly know whether to call it a salad or a soup. It is refreshing, slightly tart, very liquid, contains at least some raw vegetables, and is served very cold. In Russia, the liquid is kvass or kvass mixed with sour cream, and the soup is flavored with mustard and sugar. A similar soup is made in the Ukraine and Central Asia with soured milk. In the United States, people from these lands substitute buttermilk, yogurt, and sour cream in various combinations and dilutions. None of the substitutes is quite like the rich clabbered, soured, and cultured milks and creams of the old country. However, unless you live near an émigré farm community where someone reproduces these delights from unhomogenized (or perhaps even unpasteurized) milk and cream, you will have to make the best of what is commercially available. On page 227 are two formulas that approximate the flavor; both can substitute for kvass in Russian Okroshka too.

RUSSIAN OKROSHKA WITH MEAT

SERVINGS: 6

> ½ lb. cold leftover meat (boiled or roasted)
> 2 medium cucumbers
> 2 hard-boiled eggs
> ½ bunch spring onions
> 3 Tb sour cream
> 1 Tb prepared mustard
> ¾ tsp sugar
> 1½ recipes sour milk substitute (page 227)
> salt and ground white pepper to taste
> 3 Tb fresh minced herbs (dill, tarragon, parsley)

Cube meat and cucumbers; chop hard-boiled eggs and onions. Gradually mix sour cream with mustard and sugar. Stir in sour milk substitute and season to taste with salt and pepper. Mix all ingredients together and chill well before serving.

RUSSIAN VEGETABLE OKROSHKA

SERVINGS: 4

> 2 medium potatoes
> 1 beetroot
> 1 carrot
> 1 cucumber
> ½ bunch spring onions
> 2 Tb sour cream
> ½ tsp sugar
> 1 recipe sour-milk substitute (page 227)
> salt and ground white pepper to taste
> 2 Tb fresh minced herbs (dill, tarragon, parsley)

Boil potatoes, beetroot, and carrot separately until tender.
Let them cool. Peel potatoes and beetroot; cube all 3
vegetables. Cube cucumber; chop onions. Blend sour
cream with sugar and sour-milk substitute, season it with
salt and pepper, and mix in the vegetables and herbs.
Chill well before serving

QUICK OKROSHKA

SERVINGS: 5–6

> 2 cups cooked fresh, frozen, or canned spinach with
>   juice
> 2–3 hard-boiled eggs
> ½ cucumber, cubed
> 1 heaping Tb minced dill and parsley, combined
> ¾ tsp sugar
> 3 cups buttermilk

Chop spinach and hard-boiled eggs. Combine them
with cucumber, dill, and parsley. Stir in sugar and
buttermilk. Serve thoroughly chilled.

CHALOP

Chalop is an Uzbek soup for the parching hot summer
days. It consists almost entirely of herbs and liquid.

SERVINGS: 6

> 4 cups sour milk (or sour-milk substitute, page 227)
> 1 cup cold water
> salt and cayenne pepper to taste
> 2 medium cucumbers
> 1 bunch radishes
> ½ bunch spring onions
> 4 Tb mixed fresh herbs (parsley, dill, coriander, basil)

Mix sour milk or substitute with water. Season with salt and pepper. Clean and mince vegetables and herbs. Stir into liquid. Chill and serve very cold with a lump of ice in each plate.

FRUIT SOUP

Cold soups made from fresh and dried fruits are served as a first course in parts of the Ukraine and as a dessert farther north. Some are like a very liquid compote, with the fruit left whole or cut in pieces; others, such as the following, are purées.

SERVINGS: 6

> ¾ lb. assorted dried fruits
> ½ stick cinnamon
> 6 cups water
> ¼–½ cup sugar (to taste)
> juice of ½ lemon
> a little grated lemon rind

Wash fruit in warm water. Cover fruit and cinnamon stick with 6 cups cold water. Cook over low heat until

fruit is very soft. Remove fruit and force it through a
sieve into a serving bowl. Add sugar to taste to fruit
juice, bring it to a rolling boil, stir in lemon juice and
then mix with the puréed fruit. Chill thoroughly and
serve sprinkled with a little finely grated lemon rind.

RUSSIAN BEER SOUP

SERVINGS: 10

> 1 pint light beer
> 1 12-oz. bottle imported dark beer
> ½ stick cinnamon
> ½ cup seedless raisins
> 2 cups milk
> 2 cups light cream (half and half)
> ⅓ cup sugar
> a pinch of salt
> 1 egg, separated
> a pinch of sugar
> a sprinkling of ground cinnamon

Pour beer into a large saucepan, add cinnamon stick
and raisins, bring to a full boil, then lower heat and
simmer for 7 minutes. Set aside to cool.

When beer mixture is cool, add cold milk, cream, ⅓
cup sugar, and salt. (Do not add before beer has cooled
or the mixture will curdle.) Beat in egg yolk until smooth.
Separately, beat egg white stiff with a generous pinch
of sugar. Float egg white on top of soup like little islands
and sprinkle them with a bit of ground cinnamon.

CHAPTER FOUR

GARNISHES AND SIDE
DISHES FOR SOUPS

GARNISHES, side dishes, or both always accompany soup
in northern Russia. Some of them are part of the recipe.
The chopped dill, chopped spring onions, and cubed
meat in borshch, the bowl of sour cream on the side, the
capers and olives in Solianka—these are not extra
flourishes, but an integral part of a specific dish.

For Russians, this is not enough. There is a long list of
additional items that can be put in soup or served with
it. None of them is limited to a single recipe or essential
to it. Tradition, logic, and one's own taste guide the
choice.

The small pastries known as meat-stuffed pirozhky are
generally associated with borshch. However, a borshch
containing large chunks of meat would not be served
with meat-stuffed pirozhky, but with cabbage-stuffed
pirozhky instead, or with another dish altogether. A plate
of buckwheat kasha, a hard-boiled egg cut in half,
Grenky (cheese toast)—these are classic companions of
borshch, too. Others, less usual, are Kulebiaka (a large
meat pastry), Blinchaty Pirog (a pancake pie), and pancake rolls. In the Baltic region, people serve pirozhky
only with a clear bouillon, never with borshch.

Russian cabbage soup, or shchi, is often acompanied
by the cottage cheese tarts known as Vatrushky. Green

Shchi may have hard-boiled eggs in it or be presented
with hot stuffed eggs, while pelmeny and other dumplings are reserved for clear soups.

For convenience, the list of soup accompaniments is
divided in 2 parts: those served *in* soups and those served
as a side dish *with soups*. The latter are put on what
Russians call the pirozhnaya plate, a small dish put next
to each person's soup bowl.

All these soup accompaniments belong to areas of
Slavic influence: they are Great Russian, Ukrainian,
Belorussian, Lithuanian, Latvian, or Estonian. In the
Caucasus and Central Asia, soups are either considered
substantial enough to stand on their own or are intended
to be light, refreshing appetizers, like the cold summer
soups and tart soups with lemon and sour milk.

SOUP ACCOMPANIMENTS SERVED IN SOUP

HARD-BOILED EGGS. Chop and sprinkle over Green
Shchi before serving.

LAPSHA (noodles), page 88. To serve in soup, cut thin
and cook 2–3 minutes in boiling salt water. Drain
and complete cooking in soup. Use in clear soups
and chicken soups.

SIBERIAN PELMENY (stuffed dumplings), page 80. Cook
in soup just before it is to be served so that the
dumplings do not become too soft. Made very small,
pelmeny are sometimes called ushky.

LITHUANIAN VIRTINIAI (stuffed dumplings), pages 83–
84. Mushroom-filled dumplings are traditionally
served on Christmas Eve in a meatless beet soup.
They are delicious in plain meat bouillon, to which
they give a particularly rich flavor.

SIDE DISHES SERVED WITH SOUP

HARD-BOILED EGGS. Peel and cut in half, lengthwise. Serve with Green Shchi.

HOT STUFFED EGGS. Also good with Green Shchi.

SERVINGS: 6

> 6 eggs plus 1 egg yolk
> 5 Tb butter
> 1 Tb minced fresh green herbs (parsley, dill, tarragon)
> salt and pepper to taste
> a small pinch of sugar
> 1 Tb fine dry bread crumbs

Set oven at 450°. Hard-boil eggs and halve them lengthwise. Remove yolk, mash it, mix it with 4 Tb melted butter, 1 Tb minced herbs, salt and pepper to taste, and a small pinch of sugar. With care, enlarge the hollows of the egg whites so that they will hold more stuffing. Fill them with the egg yolk mixture, sprinkle them with bread crumbs, dot remaining butter on top, and bake on upper shelf of 450° oven about 5 minutes, or until eggs are lightly browned.

BOILED POTATOES. Cook medium-size potatoes, 1–2 per person, in boiling salt water until tender. Peel and serve with Sour Shchi.

GRENKI. Grenki are nothing more than slices of bread sprinkled with grated cheese, dotted with melted butter, and put under a broiler or on the top of a hot oven long enough to melt and brown the cheese. They go with borshch and shchi.

BUCKWHEAT KASHA, page 177. Kasha is traditional with borshch. Sometimes the cooked kasha is sprinkled with grated cheese and baked until the cheese forms a crust.

KASHA SQUARES. These are served with Green Shchi and borshch.

SERVINGS: 8

> ¾ lb. buckwheat kasha
> 3 Tb cooking oil
> boiling water with 1 tsp salt
> 3 Tb butter
> 1 egg, beaten
> ½ cup bread crumbs (approximately)

Fry kasha with oil in skillet for 15 minutes, stirring almost constantly to prevent burning. Put kasha in a saucepan and cover it, 2 fingers deep, with boiling salt water. Add 1 Tb butter and simmer 15–20 minutes or until kasha is cooked through.

Wet a rectangular baking pan with cold water. Press kasha into it with a wet spatula; spread kasha out evenly, about 1 finger deep. Let it cool.

When kasha has cooled, cut it in squares, dip them in beaten egg and then in bread crumbs, and fry them in butter.

PIROZHKY, pages 89–96. Serve meat pirozhky with cabbage soups, cabbage pirozhky with meat borshch. Serve either with a clear bouillon.

VATRUSHKY. Cottage cheese tarts, traditional with shchi of all kinds.

SERVINGS: 6 (about 1 doz. small tarts)

>1 recipe pirozhky dough (from page 90)
>2 cups (1 12-oz. carton) pot cheese
>1 tsp butter
>1 egg
>2 tsp sour cream
>a large pinch of salt
>a small pinch of sugar
>1 beaten egg

Set oven at 400°. Prepare dough, cover it, and set it aside in a cool place. Mix following 6 ingredients thoroughly with a fork. Roll out dough fairly thin on lightly floured surface. Cut out circles 3″–3½″ in diameter. Drop filling in middle of each circle from spoon. Pinch sides together firmly to form small tarts with open centers. Make filling level by flattening it with a fork. Brush both dough and filling with beaten egg. Bake tarts on greased sheet in 400° oven 15–20 minutes. Vatrushky are done when they move easily on the baking sheet and are lightly browned.

KULEBIAKA, pages 98–101. A large rectangular pastry; soup plus kulebiaka makes a meal.

LITHUANIAN LIETINIAI, page 105. Meat-stuffed pancakes, served with meat and vegetable bouillon (page 47).

BLINCHATY PIROG, page 111. A pancake pie; not a light dish, but delicious.

CHAPTER FIVE

PELMENY AND OTHER
DUMPLINGS

PELMENY are commonly known as Siberian pelmeny, not because they are a native Siberian dish, but because of the popularity they acquired in Siberia, where local food and transportation were scarce. Siberian households used to store the little half-moon or triangular meat-stuffed dumplings in earthenware jars, buried in the ice; the ice was chipped away with an axe to get at the pelmeny jars. Pelmeny were a favorite for long winter journeys along with shchi and pirozhky, kept frozen on top of the sleigh during the trip and warmed up at the night's stopping place. The pelmeny in the following recipes can be frozen in the home freezer, too.

Pelmeny is the Russian name. Similar little dumplings appear under various names in various regions, each of which has its favorite stuffings. They range from the cottage-cheese-stuffed vareniky of the Ukraine through the ground lamb and coriander dumplings of the Caucasus (dyushbara or dyushpere), and the steamed pumpkin-stuffed manty of Central Asia.

SIBERIAN PELMENY

Stuffed Russian Dumplings

Russians like to serve pelmeny in the bouillon in which they cooked, as a soup course. Siberians boil their pelmeny in so little broth that it is almost gone when the dumplings are done. The pelmeny in their concentrated broth are topped with butter and sour cream to make a first or main course.

SERVINGS: 4–6 as a main course; 10–12 as a garnish for soup

PELMENY DOUGH

1¾ cups all-purpose flour
1 egg
⅓ cup cold water
½ tsp salt
½ tsp sugar

Put flour in a large bowl and make a hollow in the center. Pour in the hollow the egg, lightly beaten, and ⅓ cup water in which sugar and salt have been dissolved. Mix thoroughly with hands. Add a little water if needed to mix in flour; add a little flour if needed to keep dough from sticking to fingers. Form a ball, cover, and set aside while preparing filling

PELMENY MEAT FILLING

1 small onion, minced (⅓ cup or more)
1–2 Tb butter
½ lb. ground chuck
salt and ground pepper to taste

Fry minced onion slowly in 1 Tb butter in covered frying pan until onion is soft and golden. Add ground meat and cook rapidly, uncovered, until meat loses red color. Stir constantly while frying meat; add butter if necessary. Season to taste with salt and pepper. Put aside to cool before stuffing dough.

COOKING AND SERVING PELMENY

8 cups canned beef bouillon*

Roll out half the dough very thin on a lightly floured surface. Cut dough with a glass 2½" in diameter or slightly larger. Place a little filling in the center of each round of dough (a ½-tsp measuring spoon is a convenient instrument). Dip finger in ice water and run it around half the dough round. Fold dry side over and pinch edges together very firmly. (It is even more important to pinch the edges firmly in making pelmeny than in making pirozhky: in the latter case, if the dough splits open, at least the filling—or most of it—will remain in place, but the pelmeny filling will spill into the broth.)

Bring bouillon to a rolling boil and drop pelmeny into it, 15–20 at a time. Cook 3–5 minutes or until done. Test frequently: overcooked pelmeny become flabby like overcooked noodles. Remove pelmeny with slotted spoon when done.

NOTE: Pelmeny can also be cut in squares about 2½ x 2½" and folded in triangles to save time.

VARENIKY WITH COTTAGE CHEESE FILLING

Stuffed Ukrainian Dumplings

These are typical of the Ukraine, where cottage cheese is the favorite filling.†

---

* Homemade stock would be wasted effort in this instance because the pelmeny give canned bouillon so much flavor that it tastes homemade.

† In the Western Ukraine, brindza cheese, which is more like the Caucasian feta cheese, is substituted for pot cheese in the filling.

SERVINGS: 4–6

  1½ cups pot cheese
  1 Tb butter
  1 egg yolk
  1 rounded tsp sour cream (more if pot cheese is very dry)
  a pinch of salt
  1 recipe Pelmeny Dough (page 80)
  ¼ cup melted butter
  a bowl of sour cream

Force pot cheese and butter through a sieve. Mix in egg yolk, sour cream, and salt. Prepare Pelmeny Dough. Roll and cut it as directed in pelmeny recipe. Fill each circle or square with the cheese, seal edges with care, and drop the dumplings, 15–20 at a time, in a large pot of boiling salt water. Remove with slotted spoon when done (3–5 minutes). Drain well. To prevent sticking, toss immediately (but gently) in melted butter. Serve hot with a bowl of sour cream on the side.

VARENIKY WITH SAUERKRAUT

Ukrainian Sauerkraut Dumplings

SERVINGS: 4–6

  1 cup sauerkraut, squeezed dry
  1 medium onion, minced
  2 Tb butter
  a pinch of sugar
  1 rounded Tb sour cream at room temperature
  1 recipe Pelmeny Dough (page 80)
  ¼ cup melted butter
  either a bowl of sour cream or 3 slices bacon

If the kraut is very sour, rinse it in water and squeeze it again. Chop it thoroughly. Fry it slowly until almost dry in a lightly greased frying pan. Separately, fry minced onion in butter until golden. Add onion and sugar to sauerkraut. Cover pan and continue cooking over low flame until sauerkraut is soft. Mix in sour cream to blend mixture.

Prepare dough and roll out as directed in recipe for pelmeny. Fill each circle or square with sauerkraut-onion mixture, pinch edges together firmly, and drop, 15–20 at a time, in a large pot of boiling salt water. Remove with slotted spoon when done (3–5 minutes), drain well, and toss gently in melted butter. Serve with a bowl of sour cream on the side or sprinkle with chopped, fried diced bacon.

VIRTINIAI

Stuffed Lithuanian Dumplings

Virtiniai are the Lithuanian version of pelmeny. Like almost all Lithuanian foods, they are served with quantities of melted butter and sour cream. When I first ate them in a Lithuanian household, I changed my mental picture of a "bowl of sour cream." Here was no soup bowl, holding, at most, a cupful, but a large tureen, filled to the brim.

The dumplings are made with various fillings. Recipes for the two most popular—mushroom and meat—are given in the following pages.

VIRTINIAI DOUGH

SERVINGS: 4–6 as a main course; 10–12 as a garnish for soup

>2 cups all-purpose flour
>1 beaten egg
>4 Tb melted butter
>4–6 Tb water
>½ tsp salt
>8 cups beef broth or salt water for cooking virtiniai

Put flour in a bowl or on a flat surface. Make a hollow in the middle and pour in all other ingredients except for 1 Tb water and the broth. Mix well. Add remaining water only if needed to bind dough together. Keep dough covered with a towel while preparing filling.

Roll dough out, making it as thin as possible without tearing. Cut circles with a small glass. Put a small amount of filling in the center of each circle, fold the dough over to form a half circle, and pinch the edges together very firmly.

To cook the dumplings, bring 8 cups of beef broth or salt water to a rolling boil, drop dumplings in, 15–20 at a time, and cook 4–6 minutes or until dough is done. Remove with slotted spoon and serve in bowls with melted butter poured over dumplings and sour cream on the side.

MUSHROOM FILLING

Mushroom dumplings are a special treat for the winter holidays and one of the traditional Lithuanian Christmas Eve dishes. Only dried wild mushrooms are used in Lithuania for lack of fresh ones during the holiday season. Every Lithuanian household has a supply of these tasty dried mushrooms, gathered in the fall and stored away for the winter.

In America, Lithuanians combine fresh mushrooms with dried. A small package (⅛–¼ oz.) of the dried mushrooms sold in Eastern European and German delicatessens will add to the flavor of the dumplings, but they are delicious with fresh mushrooms alone. Dried mushrooms should be washed and soaked overnight. The liquid, strained through fine cheesecloth to eliminate sand and grit, can be saved for sauces and soups.

SERVINGS: filling for 1 recipe Virtiniai Dough

> 1 small onion
> ⅔ lb. fresh mushrooms
> 1-2 packages dried mushrooms (optional), soaked in water overnight
> 4 Tb butter
> ¼ tsp salt
> 1 beaten egg
> 1½ tsp instant mashed potato (or 1 or more Tb leftover mashed potato)

Mince onion and mushrooms. Fry gently, covered, in 4 Tb butter until onions are soft and mushrooms dark. Mix in salt and let cool. When cool, add beaten egg and enough mashed potato to bind filling. Prepare and serve dumplings as described in preceding recipe.

NOTE: Mushroom dumplings are best small enough to be eaten in 1 bite so that none of the juice is lost from the filling. A circle 2¼″ in diameter is the smallest that can be handled with ease, and the dumplings can be somewhat larger to save time and effort.

MEAT FILLING

SERVINGS: filling for 1 recipe Virtiniai Dough

¼ lb. beef
¼ lb. veal
¼ lb. pork
1 small onion
½ tsp salt
ground black pepper to taste
¼ tsp marjoram (optional)
melted butter and sour cream to serve with dumplings

Grind raw meats with onion very coarsely; the mixture should be coarser than hamburger. Mix in seasonings. Fill dough, and boil as directed in recipe for Virtiniai Dough, but add 5–10 minutes to cooking time. Serve with melted butter and sour cream.

VARŠKIEČIAI

Lithuanian Cottage Cheese Squares

The name varškiečiai (pronounced var-skay-chay) comes from the Lithuanian word for cottage cheese, varške. In the Ukraine, they are called "Lazy Dumplings." Varškiečiai are a delicious and filling supper dish or first course. Leftovers, fried in butter the following day, are a favorite Lithuanian breakfast.

SERVINGS: 6

2 eggs
1 tsp salt
4 cups pot cheese (2 12-oz. cartons)
1¼ cups all-purpose flour (approximately)
melted butter
a bowl of sour cream

Bring a large pot of salt water to a boil while you beat the eggs lightly with 1 tsp salt. Using a fork, mix the eggs with pot cheese in a large bowl. Add 1 cup flour and blend with fingers. The dough will have undissolved lumps of cottage cheese in it; that is normal and there is no need to try to get rid of them. Continue adding flour until dough no longer sticks to fingers, but add only the minimum necessary; too much flour will make the cheese squares tough.

Form a ball of dough and divide it in 2 parts. Before rolling out dough, set oven to 250° and put out an oven-proof platter or pan in which to put the cooked Varškiečiai. Roll out one ball of dough in an oval shape ¼" thick on a lightly floured surface. With a knife, score dough diagonally across and down to make square or diamond-shaped pieces measuring about 2½" on a side. Prepare a lightly floured surface and scoop the pieces onto it so that they will not stick.

To cook them, drop a few at a time into the boiling salt water. As soon as they rise to the surface and float, they are done. Remove them with a slotted spoon, drain them well, and place in the pan or platter in the oven to keep warm.

Continue cooking the Varškiečiai while rolling out and cutting remaining dough. Serve them in shallow bowls with melted butter and sour cream on the side.

NOODLES may not be Russian in origin, but they are eaten in all parts of the Soviet Union. Whether they are called lapsha (Russian), lokshnya (Ukrainian), lagman (Uzbek) or ginei (Caucasian), and whether they are served in soup, baked in a cottage cheese casserole, or eaten alone, homemade noodles are a good dish and no more effort than homemade biscuits. The following is an Uzbek side dish of noodles.

CHUP OSHI

Uzbek Homemade Egg Noodles

SERVINGS: 4

> 1 cup all-purpose flour
> ¼ tsp salt
> 1 egg
> 6 cups meat stock or bouillon or salt water
> 1 medium-large onion, chopped
> 3 Tb butter
> ½ cup sour milk (or sour-milk substitute from page 227)
> ground black pepper to taste

Sift flour with salt. Make a hollow in the middle. Put the egg in it and mix the dough. If the dough sticks to the fingers, add a little flour. If it seems too dry, add 1 or more Tb of the meat stock. Form a ball from the dough, cover it with a towel, and let it rest 30 minutes.

Roll it out as thin as possible on a kitchen towel, turning the dough over from time to time while rolling to keep it from sticking. Leave it on the towel to dry until it is no longer sticky, but not yet brittle (1–2 hours). Roll it up loosely like a jelly roll and cut thin slices. Unroll the slices and let noodles dry out thoroughly, stretched full length on the towel (several hours).

To cook, drop noodles in rapidly boiling stock or salt water and boil 7–10 minutes or until tender.

While noodles boil, fry chopped onion in butter until golden. Strain cooked noodles thoroughly, mix with fried onion and sour milk, season with pepper to taste, and reheat to serving temperature.

CHAPTER SIX

PIROZHKY AND OTHER PASTRIES

Pirozhky are one of the best Russian foods and one of the most essential. If we are to believe Russian nineteenth-century novelists, a bourgeois household, before starting on a trip, would ensure its supply of pirozhky by devoting three days to their preparation. In one of the classic Russian fairy tales, the princess bakes the hero a batch of pirozhky to take with him when he goes to slay the wicked witch, and it is when he runs out of pirozhky that he is really in trouble.

The Russian name for these little turnovers comes from the old word for feast: *pir*. There are many derivatives of this word in Russian: pirozhnoye means pastry in general, pirozhok is the singular of pirozhky, and a pirog is a large covered pastry.

In America, very small pirozhky are sometimes passed as cocktail appetizers. In Russia, small ones may be on the zakusky table, but it is more common to serve them with soup. The size of the pastry depends on whether you are using it as an appetizer (3″ or less in length) or a soup accompaniment (5″ or more). Almost all Russian recipes say "cut the pirozhky with a glass." That is about it, but use a shot glass for the cocktail pastries and an outsize old-fashioned glass for those served with soup.

The doughs used for pirozhky and for the larger

kulebiaka are varied, interchangeable, and—with the exception of those containing sour cream—not particularly Russian or even Slavic in origin. Any dough suitable for turnovers can be used. The ones given in the following chapter were chosen because they are relatively easy and quickly made.

All pirozhky can be frozen and reheated for use. To heat, place pirozhky in aluminum foil with a few drops of water. Close foil with care and leave in 400° oven about 15 minutes.

PIROZHKY WITH SOUR-CREAM DOUGH

These are Ukrainian pirozhky, meant to accompany Ukrainian Borshch II (page 49) and to be made from the soup meat.

SERVINGS: about 60 pirozhky

DOUGH

¾ lb. butter
6 cups sifted all-purpose flour
3 egg yolks
1 tsp salt
2 cups sour cream* (aproximately)
1 beaten egg

Crumble butter and flour together with fingertips. Stir in egg yolks lightly beaten with salt. Add enough sour cream (approximately 2 cups) to make a dough that can be rolled easily. Chill dough for at least 1 hour before rolling out.

---

* Preferably rich sour cream made from whipping cream (see page 226).

Set oven at 350°. Roll dough out on lightly floured surface. Cut it in large circles (about 5" in diameter), place filling in middle, fold over and pinch edges together very firmly with fingers or press them together with a fork dipped in flour. Brush pastries with beaten egg, prick top crust with fork, and bake them in 350° oven on a lightly greased baking sheet 20–25 minutes, or until browned. Serve hot.

MEAT FILLING

2 medium onions, chopped
2 Tb bacon fat
3 lbs. boiled beef
4 hard-boiled eggs (optional)
1 cup beef broth or consommé (approximately)
salt and pepper to taste

Fry chopped onion in bacon fat until onion is transparent. Grind meat, mix with onion and chopped hard-boiled eggs, if eggs are to be used. Add enough beef broth to moisten filling, and season it with salt and pepper to taste.

QUICK PIROZHKY WITH CREAM CHEESE DOUGH AND CABBAGE STUFFING

While not traditional in Russia, cream cheese is a short-cut to a rich dough, quicker to mix than the usual short pastry. Because Russians use all kinds of foreign pastries in baking, I see no reason not to adopt this quick formula.

Consisting mainly of cream cheese and butter, the dough must be kept cool. It should be mixed quickly and chilled a bit before being rolled out. On a very hot day, it is best to mix it in the cool of the morning.

SERVINGS: Dough for 40 small pirozhky (2¾" circles)

¼ lb. lightly salted butter
6 oz. cream cheese
¼ tsp salt
1 cup plus 2 Tb flour
1 egg white

Leave butter outside refrigerator ½ hour before starting recipe. Preheat oven to 350°.

Beat butter with cream and salt. Add unsifted flour and knead rapidly. Dough should have just enough flour to keep it from sticking to fingers: add a little more if necessary. Form a ball, wrap it in wax paper, and chill it in the refrigerator 15 minutes (longer if kitchen is warm). When ready to use, roll out rapidly on lightly floured surface. Cut pirozhky with a small glass. After stuffing them and pinching edges together with fingers or floured fork, brush dough with white of egg. Bake about 25 minutes or until golden brown in 350° oven.

CABBAGE FILLING FOR PIROZHKY

½ small compact head of white cabbage
3 Tb lightly salted butter
½ tsp salt
¼ tsp sugar
2 hard-boiled eggs
½ tsp lightly salted butter, melted

Shred cabbage fine. Drop into boiling water for 1 minute. Drain and rinse in cold water. Squeeze cabbage hard, handful by handful, to eliminate all water. Cook it slowly over low heat in 3 Tb butter for about 20 minutes (or until it is soft but not completely limp). Stir frequently while cooking.

When cabbage is soft, mix in salt, sugar, finely

chopped hard-boiled eggs, and melted butter. Cool filling before stuffing dough.

PIROZHKY WITH SHORT PASTRY AND CHICKEN-AND-LIVER FILLING

SERVINGS: 20 small pirozhky (3" circles)

DOUGH

1½ cups sifted all-purpose flour
½ tsp salt
¼ tsp baking powder
½ cup butter
¼ cup cold water (approximately)
1 beaten egg or beaten egg white or yolk

Preheat oven to 400°. Sift dry ingredients together. Cut in butter with pastry blender or 2 knives until mixture is evenly distributed in tiny balls. Add enough water to make mixture hold together. Roll dough out on lightly floured surface. With a glass, cut into circles 3" in diameter. Place filling in center, fold dough over, and press edges together with floured fork. Brush with egg, place on greased sheet, and bake until golden brown (about 15 minutes).

CHICKEN-AND-LIVER FILLING

1 onion, minced
2 Tb butter
1 lb. beef lungs, boiled
2 chicken livers, broiled
1 cup cooked chicken
1 egg, beaten
salt and pepper to taste

Fry onion slowly in butter until soft and golden. Chop lungs, livers, and chicken. Mix in onion, butter, egg, salt, and pepper; blend well and fill pirozhky.

PIROZHKY WITH PACKAGED DOUGH AND SPICY MEAT FILLING

Small meat pirozhky need a well-flavored filling. In Russia, part of the flavor comes from a heavy use of dill and part from the addition of strong beef bouillon (always on hand in the ubiquitous pot of soup). In America, where the bouillon is not often homemade and fresh dill is not always available, cooks have looked for new sources of flavor. The following recipe for spicy meat filling and packaged dough makes delicious pirozhky in the new tradition.

DOUGH

2 cylindrical packages refrigerated, unbaked crescent rolls
a small bowl of ice water
1 egg white

Preheat oven to 350°. Cut each package of rolls into 14 slices. On a lightly floured board, roll each slice into a circle approximately 3½″ in diameter. Patch any holes that appear with bits of dough dipped in ice water.

Put 1 heaping tsp stuffing in the center of each circle. Dip finger in ice water and wet the edge of half the circle of dough. Fold the dry half over and pinch the edges together firmly and thoroughly. Place the pirozhky on a greased baking sheet. Repeat for the remaining pirozhky.

Beat the egg white lightly with a fork. Brush the

pirozhky with the beaten egg white and bake them in a 350° oven for about 20 minutes or until nicely browned.

SPICY MEAT FILLING

1 small onion, minced
2 Tb butter
1 lb. ground chuck
½ tsp Worcestershire sauce
1 tsp beef extract
½ tsp salt
⅛ tsp ground black pepper

Fry onion gently in butter until golden. Add ground beef and continue to fry, stirring frequently, until meat loses red color. Mix in remaining ingredients, remove from fire, and set aside to cool before filling dough.

DEEP-FRIED PIROZHKY

SERVINGS: 18–20 large pirozhky to serve with soup

DOUGH

3½–4 cups all-purpose flour
4 Tb baking powder
1½ tsp salt
1 tsp sugar
2 eggs
1 cup milk
3 Tb melted butter
3–4 cups oil for deep frying

Sift 3½ cups flour with baking powder, salt, and sugar. Beat eggs, milk, and melted butter lightly and mix in dry ingredients. Add a little more flour if necessary to make dough firm enough to handle. Put in a bowl, cover with a towel, and chill before rolling out.

Roll out rather thin on lightly floured surface. Cut in circles about 5″ in diameter (the circles will shrink after cutting). Put a rounded Tb of filling on each, pinch edges together with fingers or press together with floured fork. Wetting fingers slightly, press edges flat and form pirozhky into a slightly flattened oval shape. Smooth dough with wet fingers. As they are formed, place the pirozhky on a floured surface. Let them sit while heating the oil.

When the oil is hot, but not so hot that it will brown the pirozhky at once, lower them in carefully, a few at a time, and fry them until brown on all sides, turning when necessary. Drain on paper towels and serve hot.

NOTE: These can be cooked in advance and reheated for 15–20 minutes in a paper bag in a 400° oven.

FILLING

Use Cabbage Filling (page 92) or ½ recipe of one of the kulebiaka meat stuffings on page 100.

PARAMACH

Fried Tartar Meat Pastries

When Tartars make these delectable pastries, they serve them with no more than a salad on the side and follow them only with tea. As they explained to me, when you have eaten all the paramach you want, you want nothing more; and they are quite right.

SERVINGS: 4–6 generous portions (a total of about 18
          paramach)

DOUGH

2 tsp vegetable oil
1⅓ cups cold milk
2 tsp baking powder
1 tsp salt
1½ tsp sugar
2¾–3 cups all-purpose flour

FILLING

1½ lbs. lean ground beef
2 small onions, coarsely grated
2 small garlic cloves, coarsely grated
1 tsp salt
2 tsp flour
¼ tsp ground black pepper
1½ cups vegetable oil for frying

For the dough, add oil to milk, sift baking powder, salt,
sugar, and 2¾ cups flour over liquids, and blend well.
The dough should be soft, but add more flour if necessary to make it easy to handle. Cover and set aside for
½ hour to rise. Mix all ingredients for filling.

Divide dough into small balls, each about the size of
a golf ball. Roll each out in an even circle about 5″ in
diameter and as thin as a thin china plate. The outer
edges should, if possible, be even thinner* because they
will be gathered together later.

Leaving a margin of ¾″ all around, spread the filling
thickly on each round of dough. Gently bend the edges
of the dough over the meat and gather them together,
pinching them between thumb and forefinger to make

---

* Tartars prefer a rolling pin that narrows at either end. By
using the sloping ends, they make edges of pastry thinner than
the middle with ease. Rolling pins of this kind are sold in the
Chinese districts of large cities.

them stick. The center of the little meat pie will remain uncovered.

Pour cooking oil in a frying pan to a level of about ⅜". (A heavy cast-iron skillet is best for this dish.) When the oil is hot enough to fry quickly, but is not yet smoking, put the meat pies in, a few at a time, open side down. Using 2 long forks, turn them as soon as they are browned. When they are browned on both sides, remove them and drain on absorbent paper.

Paramach are usually served hot with a little hot bouillon poured over the meat through the opening. They can also be served with a little horseradish or sour cream or soy sauce.

KULEBIAKA

A kulebiaka is a large square, rectangular, or bread-shaped pastry, usually stuffed with meat. Like most Russian food, it is delicious reheated and seems to improve from day to day. You will never regret having made a large one. An excellent buffet dish, it can be baked in the morning and put in a 400° oven for 15–20 minutes to reheat just before serving time.

Various doughs are used for kulebiaka; any dough suitable for baked pirozhky is suitable for kulebiaka, too. The following is a rich short pastry.

SERVINGS: a large kulebiaka for 10–12

KULEBIAKA DOUGH

4½–5 cups all-purpose flour
1 tsp salt
1 tsp sugar
½ lb. butter
¼ cup sour cream
3 whole eggs, lightly beaten
1 egg yolk mixed with 1 tsp water

Preheat oven to 350°. Sift 4½ cups flour with salt and sugar into a large bowl. Add butter cut into small pieces. Blend with fingertips until butter is fairly evenly distributed through flour. Add sour cream and 3 lightly beaten eggs. Knead dough until it is well blended. It should be firm, but not difficult to work. If it is too soft, add a little more sifted flour (probably ½ cup or less). Place dough on a flat surface and blend more thoroughly by alternately pushing dough with heel of hand and folding it over.

There are 2 methods of rolling out kulebiaka. Following the first method, divide dough in 2 parts, one of them slightly larger than the other. Roll out the smaller in a rectangle and put it on a greased baking sheet. Heap the filling on the rectangle and press the filling into a loaf shape, leaving ½″ margin of uncovered dough all around. Roll out the larger ball of dough to cover the filling. With wet hands, pinch the sides together very firmly. Brush dough with 1 egg yolk mixed with 1 tsp water Prick the top in several places with a fork and bake the kulebiaka 30–40 minutes or until nicely browned in a 350° oven.

In the second method, the kulebiaka dough is rolled out in a single large rectangle. The filling is heaped on half of it and patted into a mound, leaving a ½″ margin on 3 of the sides. The uncovered portion of dough is folded over the filling, the edges are pinched together as described above, and the entire kulebiaka is carefully rolled onto a greased baking sheet in such a way that the seam is on the bottom. The kulebiaka is reshaped with wet hands, and then brushed with egg and baked as in the first method.

RICH MEAT STUFFING FOR KULEBIAKA

2 medium onions, chopped fine
¼ lb. butter
3 lbs. boiled soup beef
several Tb beef bouillon or meat stock
1½–2 tsp salt (to taste)
¼ tsp ground black pepper
4 hard-boiled eggs
4 Tb minced fresh dill and parsley, mixed

Fry chopped onions slowly, covered, until very soft in 3 Tb butter. While onions fry, put meat through course grinder. Melt remaining butter and mix it with meat and onions. If necessary to moisten mixture in order to make it stick together, add a little bouillon. Season mixture to taste with salt and pepper.

In a separate bowl, mix chopped hard-boiled eggs with minced dill and parsley. Fill kulebiaka dough with alternate layers of the meat mixture and the egg-herb mixture.

NOTE: The meat, onion, eggs, and herbs can be mixed together if preferred.

LEAN-MEAT STUFFING FOR KULEBIAKA

2 medium onions, chopped fine
2 Tb melted butter
1 Tb cooking oil
3 lbs. boiled soup beef
1½–1¾ cups beef bouillon
salt and pepper to taste
4 hard-boiled eggs
4 Tb minced dill and parsley, mixed

Fry onions slowly, covered, until very soft in a mixture of 2 Tb butter and 1 Tb cooking oil. While onions fry, put meat through coarse grinder. Mix meat with onions, add enough bouillon to make the mixture stick together, and season it to taste with salt and pepper. In a separate bowl, mix chopped hard-boiled eggs with minced dill and parsley. Continue as in preceding recipe.

GROUND-MEAT STUFFING FOR KULEBIAKA

3 onions, chopped fine
5–6 Tb butter
3 lbs. ground beef chuck
5 hard-boiled eggs
3 Tb minced parsley (or dill and parsley combined)
salt and ground black pepper to taste

Fry chopped onion gently in 2 Tb butter until transparent. Add ground meat and continue frying with frequent stirring until all meat has lost red color. Remove from fire, pour off a little of the grease if the meat is very fat, and mix in remaining ingredients. Add enough melted butter (3–4 Tb) to make stuffing stick together.

CHAPTER SEVEN

BLINY AND OTHER
PANCAKES

BLINY are yeast-raised pancakes and the most popular kind in Russia. They can be served as a first course, a main course, or a dessert, depending on the flavoring in the dough and what is served with them. They are most often a first course, accompanied by melted butter, sour cream, and either caviar or smoked salmon. They can also be folded over stuffing, rolled around it, or made into a kind of layer cake or pancake pie with the stuffing between the layers.

Blinchiky is the Russian diminutive of bliny. The pancakes are not only smaller, they are of a thinner, unleavened batter, much like the French crêpe. The same pancake is made in Lithuania and the Ukraine under other names. Russian Blinchiky are usually a dessert pancake; Ukrainian Nalysnyky can be made with sweet or savory stuffings, and the recipe given in this chapter for Lithuanian Lietiniai serves as both main dish or soup accompaniment. Sirnichky are a Ukrainian specialty (although made by Russians, who call them tvorozhniky), and cottage cheese Oladky are similar, but lighter.

BLINY

The following recipe was given me by a Belorussian man who gets up two hours earlier than the rest of the family every Sunday morning to prepare bliny for the family breakfast. Although a kind of pancake, bliny are not usually served for breakfast, but for lunch or as a first course at dinner. They are good at any time.

The recipe cannot be made as successfully in smaller quantity, but leftovers present no problem. Unless you want to use the batter to make more bliny the following day, you can make it into a delicious fruit coffee cake. The recipe, given on page 209, was supplied by the same Belorussian.

SERVINGS: 8 generous servings or 4 servings of bliny and 1
           round coffee cake (9" in diameter)

4 Tb butter
2½ cups milk
3 cups sifted all-purpose flour
3 Tb sugar
1 tsp salt
3 eggs
1 pkg dry yeast dissolved in ¼ cup warm water
butter for frying bliny
*melted butter, sour cream, and caviar or smoked
    salmon to serve with them*

Add 4 Tb butter to milk, scald milk, and set pan in cold water to cool. Sift flour, sugar, and salt together. Beat eggs by hand in a large earthenware or pyrex bowl. Stir in cooled milk and butter with wooden spoon. Gradually incorporate the sifted dry ingredients. It does not matter if the batter is somewhat lumpy. Dissolve yeast in warm water and stir into batter. Cover with kitchen towel and let rise for 1 hour in warm spot.* Beat batter vigorously with a wooden spoon, cover it again, and let it rise for at least ½ hour or until it reaches its previous height.

Make bliny by dropping batter from a dipper onto a hot, lightly buttered surface. Bliny are usually about 5″ in diameter. The griddle should be hot enough to brown the bliny on 1 side in 40–50 seconds. When browned on both sides, stack bliny on warm plate in warm oven. Serve at once with melted butter, a dish of sour cream, and a bowl of caviar or a platter of thin slices of smoked salmon.

Store leftover batter in the refrigerator; let it come to room temperature and rise a little before using.

NOTE: Some Russians like ground black pepper and lemon with this kind of bliny as well. Another way of serving the bliny is to put a line of red caviar, a line of minced hard-boiled egg, a line of sour cream, and a line of finely minced onion on each one and roll it up.

LIETINIAI

Lithuanian Meat-stuffed Pancakes

Lietiniai are intended to be a side dish for bouillon, made simultaneously: the meat from the bouillon is used to stuff the pancakes served with it. Most people will find the pancakes hearty enough for a main dish.

---

* If there is no warm room, spread a towel over a radiator and put the covered bowl of batter on it.

SERVINGS: 6

BATTER

4 eggs
1 tsp salt
¼ cup melted butter
¾ cup milk
¾ cup all-purpose flour
2–3 Tb unsalted butter for frying pancakes
3 strips bacon (optional) for topping

Beat eggs in a bowl with salt. Add melted butter and
milk to eggs. Gradually mix in flour. The batter should
be quite liquid, like a French crêpe.

Put a small dab of butter in the frying pan and melt it
over low heat. Make the pancakes, 1 at a time, by pouring a small amount of batter into the pan and immediately
spreading it about by moving the pan. There should be
just enough batter to coat the surface of the pan, and the
pan should not be so hot that the batter cooks before you
can spread it. Turn the pancake over almost immediately
and remove it when it is barely done: if it is not limp,
it will be impossible to fold. The underside can be almost
raw.

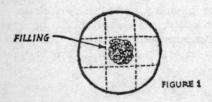

FIGURE 1

When all the pancakes are made, put stuffing in the
center of each as shown in Figure 1, and fold the sides
over the filling. Add a little more butter to the frying
pan and put the pancakes back in it, folded side down.
The cooking is completed at this stage, and the pancakes

made brown and crisp. Lithuanians like them with diced fried bacon sprinkled on top.

FILLING

1 lb. boiled meat
2 medium onions, coarsely chopped
2 hard-boiled eggs
salt and pepper to taste
¼–½ cup meat bouillon

Grind the meat once, then grind it again with the chopped onions and hard-boiled eggs. Season with salt and pepper and add ¼–½ cup bouillon if the mixture is dry.

UKRAINIAN NALYSNYKY

SERVINGS: 6

3 cups pot cheese
3 Tb butter
1 egg, lightly beaten
1–2 Tb sour cream
salt to taste
1 recipe lietiniai batter (page 105)
2–3 Tb unsalted butter for frying pancakes
a bowl of sour cream

Force cheese through sieve with butter. Mix with egg and 1–2 Tb sour cream (2 Tb if pot cheese is extremely dry). Add salt to taste.

Preheat oven to 375°. Make batter and fry pancakes as in preceding recipe, but fry on 1 side only. Roll filling in pancakes, placing filling on fried side. Put pancakes in a buttered casserole, dot top with butter, and leave in 375° oven until heated through (about 5 minutes). Serve with sour cream.

NOTE: These can also be folded and fried as in the preceding recipe; they then resemble blintzes without sugar.

SIRNICHKY

Ukrainian Cottage Cheese Patties

SERVINGS: 4 (16 small patties)

>   2 cups pot cheese (1 12-oz. carton)
>   2 eggs
>   a large pinch of salt
>   ½ cup all-purpose flour (approximately)
>   2–3 Tb butter for frying
>   a bowl of sour cream

Force cheese through sieve with wooden spoon. Beat in 2 eggs, salt, and about 6 Tb flour (use just enough to make it possible to shape the mass into patties).

Using wet hands, make small patties and dip in remaining flour, sprinkled on flat surface. Fry them, 5–6 at a time, in 1–2 Tb hot (but not browned) butter. Add butter as needed. Remove patties to warmed platter when they are browned on both sides. Serve them hot with a bowl of sour cream.

SWEET SIRNICHKY

For dessert, add 1 Tb sugar to Sirnichky batter and serve them with a bowl of sugar or jam in addition to the sour cream.

RUSSIAN BLINCHIKY

SERVINGS: 6

1 recipe lietiniai batter (page 105)
1 Tb sugar for batter
1 cup thick jam
1 egg white, lightly beaten
2–3 Tb unsalted butter for frying pancakes
2–3 Tb sugar to sprinkle over pancakes
a bowl of sour cream

Make batter as for lietiniai, but add 1 Tb sugar to it. Fry the pancakes in the same way as the lietiniai, but fry them on 1 side only and make them 3″ in diameter. Put a little jam on the fried side, fold over as for lietiniai, and seal edges with lightly beaten white of egg. Fry in unsalted butter, seam side first. Serve sprinkled with sugar with a bowl of sour cream on the side.

ROLLED BLINCHIKY

SERVINGS: 6

1 recipe lietiniai batter (page 105)
1 Tb sugar for batter
1 cup creamed cottage cheese
sugar to taste for filling
2–3 Tb unsalted batter for frying pancakes
2–3 Tb powdered sugar to sprinkle over pancakes

Preheat oven to 375°. Make batter, adding 1 Tb sugar with the flour. Fry pancakes as for lietiniai. Mix sugar to taste with creamed cottage cheese (do not drain or press it). Put a line of filling across the least browned side of each pancake and roll it up. Bake 5 minutes in 350° oven. Serve hot, sprinkled with powdered sugar.

NOTE: The same blinchiky can be filled with applesauce sweetened with cinnamon and sugar. Serve with sour cream and sugar in separate bowls.

OLADKY

Cottage Cheese Fritters

SERVINGS: 6 (about 30 fritters)

    2 cups pot cheese (1 12-oz. carton)
    2 egg yolks
    1 Tb sugar
    ½ cup plus 2 Tb all-purpose flour
    a pinch of salt
    ½ cup sour cream
    1 egg white
    3 Tb butter for frying
    a bowl of sugar
    a bowl of sour cream

Force cheese through sieve with wooden spoon. Beat egg yolks with sugar until thick. Blend into cheese. Mix in flour sifted with salt; add sour cream, and, lastly, 1 stiffly beaten egg white.

Heat 1–2 Tb butter in a frying pan. Drop batter in off the end of a large spoon. Flatten fritters by tapping lightly with the back of a spatula. Fry over medium heat, taking care not to let butter brown. Add butter as needed. Remove fritters when well browned on both sides and keep on warm platter while frying remainder.

Serve hot with a bowl of sugar and a bowl of sour cream on the side.

BLINCHATY PIROG

Pancake Pie

SERVINGS: 8

> *1½ lbs. boiled beef*
> *2 hard-boiled eggs*
> *1 small onion, minced*
> *¼ lb. butter*
> *2 eggs, lightly beaten*
> *2–3 heaping Tb fresh chopped parsley (and dill if available)*
> *½ cup beef bouillon (approximately)*
> *salt and pepper to taste*
> *2 Tb fine dry bread crumbs*
> *1 recipe lietiniai batter (page 105)*

Preheat oven to 350°. Put beef and hard-boiled eggs through grinder. Fry minced onion in 1 Tb butter. Reserving 1 Tb of the 2 lightly beaten eggs, mix eggs, onion, and fresh herbs with meat. Pour in 2 Tb melted butter and as much beef bouillon as needed to make the filling moist enough to spread easily. Season with salt and pepper to taste.

Butter a casserole the diameter of your frying pan and sprinkle the sides and bottom with 1 Tb fine bread crumbs. Make batter and fry pancakes in butter as described in lietiniai recipe, but fry them on 1 side only. As you fry, start filling the casserole. Put the first thin pancake on the bottom, browned side up. Spread a layer of filling over it. Continue, alternating pancakes and filling, until all filling is gone. Top with a pancake.

Brush the pancake with the remaining Tb of beaten egg, sprinkle it with remaining bread crumbs, and pour 2 Tb melted butter on top. Bake in a 350° oven 30–40 minutes or until browned. Unmold to serve by turning upside down over a plate.

NOTE: Blinchaty Pirog can be made with any filling you choose: chopped mushroom or chopped chicken in a thick cream sauce, for example. Some Russians serve a bowl of sour cream with it.

CHAPTER EIGHT

FISH

RUSSIA is rich in fish, with delicious sturgeon and salmon in many varieties. There are dozens of species limited to specific areas—Siberian rivers, the Black Sea, and the Baltic Sea, in particular. The most characteristic Russian ways of serving fish are with sauce sharpened with horse-radish or mustard, with sour-cream sauce, and with capers and pickles as in fish with Tartar sauce or Solianka. Dill is a favorite herb for fish and almost always included in fish recipes. Smoked salmon, sturgeon and eel; canned anchovies, sardines and sprats; herring and various kinds of caviar are used extensively in first courses as part of the zakusky. Herring appears in salads (such as Rossolye, page 38), and pancakes (Bliny) with caviar or smoked salmon are very popular (page 104).

Fresh sturgeon appears frequently in Russian recipes. In the United States, sturgeon is almost always sold directly to smokehouses by wholesale dealers. Smoked sturgeon, in my opinion, is a bit dry and far from the best of smoked fishes. Fresh, however, it is a delicately flavored, very firm white fish that lends itself to simple or elaborate treatment. Sometimes a whole sturgeon can be bought from a wholesaler through a fish store. The price will then be—or should be—surprisingly low per pound. The fish will weigh upward of 10 pounds, but

with it, you can make two recipes at once, both of which
will keep for days in the refrigerator.

STURGEON IN ASPIC

The following recipe is only as good as the fish. Unless
you can be certain the sturgeon will be impeccably fresh,
substitute another fish. Any firm white fish will do;
swordfish is particularly suitable.

Whether you have a whole fish or not, with 4–5 pounds
of it, you can make both fish in aspic and Solianka, a fish
soup that makes a delectable and substantial first course
for a later occasion.

To make both recipes at once, cook the entire amount
of fish as described below, but use for the aspic only the
firm middle part that is easier to cut in even slices. Save
the rest for the fish soup, along with fish stock not needed
for the aspic. Even the soup greens serve twice: after
you have strained the fish stock for the aspic, mash the
greens, return them to the remaining stock for the soup,
and complete the soup as described in the recipe on
page 63.

SERVINGS: 6–8 (an 8″ x 12″ ray of aspic)

> *3 lbs. sturgeon, swordfish, or other firm white fish*
> *1 fish head, if available (fish heads can often be had from fish stores for the asking)*
> *water to cover (7 cups or more)*
> *soup greens (preferably all, and in any case most, of the following): 1 celery top, 1 leek, 1 turnip, 1 parsnip, 1 carrot, 2–3 sprigs dill, 2–3 sprigs parsley*
> *1 Tb salt*
> *6 peppercorns*
> *1 bay leaf*
> *2 eggs*
> *1 carrot*
> *1 package gelatin*
> *½ cup cold water*
> *½ can beef bouillon with gelatin added*
> *salt to taste and an equal amount of sugar*

If the fish is whole, have head removed and cleaned, tail removed, scales cut off, and body of fish cleaned, but left in 1 piece with skin. Wash head and tail of fish in cold water, tie up securely in cheesecloth, and put in a large pot with what you judge will be enough water to cover all the ingredients (7–10 cups). Tie dill, celery top, and parsley together, and add them to the pot with the other cleaned soup greens, salt, peppercorns, and bay leaf. Simmer slowly, covered, 45–60 minutes.

While stock simmers, hard-boil and peel the eggs. Cook a carrot, cleaned and cut in 3 pieces, in boiling salt water until tender. As soon as carrot is tender, rinse it in cold water.

When the fish head and soup greens have cooked their allotted time, wash remaining fish, soak it in cold water 5 minutes, and tie it in cheesecloth. Drop fish into hot fish stock and cook until done. Test after 12 minutes: if the flesh is rosy and shiny, the fish is not yet cooked.

Remove cooked fish to a platter on which it can drain

and cool. When it is room temperature, take off the cheesecloth and the skin. Cut fish crosswise in slices ¼″–⅜″ thick, and cut those pieces into ½″ squares as evenly as possible. Remove any small bones or tough flesh clinging to the underside of the fish slices.

Arrange the squares of fish in a shallow (1½″–2″ high) glass baking dish approximately 8″ x 12″. Cover pieces of fish with hard-boiled eggs, sliced very thin, and decorate with paper-thin slices of carrot. Slice ½ lemon as thinly as possible and quarter the slices. Distribute these over the platter of fish.

Dissolve 1 package gelatin in ½ cup cold water. Stir into it 1½ cups hot fish stock and ½ can beef bouillon. Salt mixture to taste and add the same amount of sugar (about ¼–½ tsp). Add juice of ½ lemon (more if you prefer). Taking care to pour between the pieces of fish so that the pattern is not disturbed, pour all the liquid into the platter. The liquid should be deep enough to come about ¼″ above the fish slices. Chill in refrigerator and serve with lemon wedges and Hot Horseradish Sauce #1 or #2 (page 174).

FISH ON A SPIT

This is a fish shashlik, simple and very good. Russians usually use sturgeon; any firm white fish, such as swordfish can be substituted.

SERVINGS: 6

3 lbs. steaks cut from firm white fish in very thick
    slices
salt
2–3 spring onions
a few sprigs of fresh parsley
1 lemon

Wash cleaned fish and cut it into chunks the size of stewing meat. Salt the pieces and thread them on 6 skewers, 4–5 pieces per skewer. Place them under a hot broiler or over glowing coals. Turning frequently, brown fish on all sides until done (5–10 minutes, depending on the fish and the size of the pieces). Serve on skewers, sprinkled with minced spring onion and parsley, with lemon wedges on the side.

FRESH SALMON WITH HORSERADISH

SERVINGS: 6

> a 3-lb. piece of fresh salmon with scales removed
> salt
> 1 stalk celery
> 1 leek
> 2 onions
> 1 bay leaf
> a pinch of black pepper
> a few sprigs of fresh parsley and dill (if available)

Wash salmon, sprinkle it with salt, and let it stand 1 hour in a cool place. Bring remaining ingredients to a boil in what you judge will be enough water to cover the fish when it is added. Simmer at least 45 minutes; allow to cool.

Wrap salmon in cheesecloth, put it in the cooled bouillon, and bring it to a boil over a high fire. As soon as it boils, cover the pot and reduce heat to a simmer. Cook until fish is done through. Although it will probably need to cook longer, test it after 8–10 minutes to avoid overcooking.

Remove fish with the aid of the cheesecloth. Take off the cloth and serve the fish, cold or hot, with prepared horseradish.

FRESH SALMON WITH SOUR-CREAM SAUCE

SERVINGS: 6

> *a 3-lb. piece of fresh salmon with scales removed*
> *salt*
> *1 stalk celery*
> *1 leek*
> *2 onions*
> *1 bay leaf*
> *a pinch of black pepper*
> *a few sprigs of parsley (dill if available)*
> *1 Tb butter*
> *1 rounded Tb flour*
> *1 cup sour cream at room temperature*
> *2 Tb chopped fresh parsley (and dill, if available)*
> *ground white pepper*

Prepare salmon by sprinkling it with salt and letting it stand 1 hour in a cool place. Cook it in a bouillon made of the celery, leek, onions, bay leaf, black pepper, and herbs as described in the preceding recipe. When the fish is done, remove it from the bouillon, drain it well, and keep it on a warmed serving platter in a warm oven.

Melt butter, blend in flour, and cook them together while stirring for 1 minute. Continuing to stir, pour in 2 cups of the liquid in which the fish cooked. Stir as often as necessary to keep mixture from sticking or forming lumps while it thickens over fire. When it has thickened, remove it from the fire, add a bit of it to the sour cream, and stir that back into the sauce with the chopped herbs. Season with salt and ground white pepper to taste. Return it to the fire, let it boil once, pour it over the fish, and serve it.

WHITE FISH IN MUSHROOM SAUCE

SERVINGS: 6

> 6 center slices of any white fish
> salt
> 1½ cups water
> 1 medium onion, sliced thin
> 3–4 Tb butter
> ½ lb. mushrooms, sliced
> 2 Tb flour
> ½ cup sour cream
> salt to taste

Salt fish lightly and let stand 1 hour. Wrap it in cheese-cloth and simmer gently in water to cover (1½ cups or more). While fish cooks, fry sliced onion in 1½ Tb butter until very soft. Separately, fry sliced mushrooms in an equal amount of butter. Add butter as needed while frying. Set oven to 350°.

When both mushrooms and onions are soft, combine them and sprinkle with 2 Tb flour. Drain cooked fish and set aside. Strain 1¼ cups liquid from the cooking of the fish and blend into vegetable mixture. Continue stirring sauce over medium flame until it thickens. Cool it slightly before adding sour cream. Salt sauce to taste, pour it over fish, and reheat in 350° oven before serving.

BAKED FILLETS OF SOLE WITH MUSTARD AND SOUR-CREAM SAUCE

SERVINGS: 6

> 6 fillets of sole or flounder
> salt and white pepper
> juice of ½ lemon
> ¼ cup of water
> 1 recipe Hot-Mustard and Sour-Cream Sauce (p. 170)

Preheat oven to 350°. Wash and dry fish, sprinkle with salt and pepper, place in buttered dish, pour in lemon juice and water and cover dish with buttered paper. Bake 10–15 minutes or until done.

Serve with Hot Mustard and Sour-Cream Sauce on the side.

HALIBUT IN HORSERADISH SAUCE

SERVINGS: 6

> 6 large center slices of halibut, fresh cod, or any firm white fish
> salt
> 1½ cups* water or fish stock or vegetable bouillon made as in recipe for Fresh Salmon with Horseradish (p. 117)
> 2 Tb butter
> 2 Tb flour
> 4 Tb instant or dried horseradish, diluted according to directions

Sprinkle fish lightly with salt and let it stand 1 hour in a cool place.

Wrap fish in cheesecloth and place it in a saucepan with water, stock or bouillon. Simmer until fish is just cooked through (7–12 minutes, depending on thickness of slices).

When fish is almost done, melt butter over low fire, stir in flour, cook while stirring for 2 minutes, then blend in diluted horseradish. Drain cooked fish and put on warm platter in low oven. Strain 1½ cups of liquid from the cooking of the fish into the butter-flour mixture while stirring. Continue stirring over low fire until sauce thickens. Pour it over fish and serve.

---

* Use more if needed to cover fish.

CHAPTER NINE

FOWL

GAME is abundant in Russia, and game recipes are both imaginative and numerous: hazel hen in sour cream, wild duck in walnut sauce, or wild goose with bacon and mushrooms. There are also many ways of preparing turkey—stuffed with rice pilaf, with kasha (page 179, note), or, in the Ukraine, with the bread or apple and raisin dressings familiar to Americans. Goose and duck stuffed with apples and prunes and served with quantities of sauerkraut are popular holiday dishes in the north.

Today there are more Russian chicken recipes than ever before. Once a great delicacy, chicken has become a readily available and economic meat. Some dishes that used to be made of game, such as Pozharsky Cutlets, are now made with chicken.

Stuffed chicken breasts used to be a highly aristocratic dish and chefs lavished their imagination on new ways of serving them. The most famous and one of the most widely know Russian dishes is Kiev Cutlets, Kievskiye, Kotlety, or Côtelettes à la Kiev—the various names under which these butter-stuffed chicken breasts appear on menus. Whether they are truly Russian is debatable. As the name indicates, they originated in the Ukrainian city of Kiev. They are quick and easy to make, providing small, tender chicken breasts are available. The breasts must be small and tender or they will look clumsy and will not cook through before the butter melts.

That is the feat in the Kiev Cutlet: to get the chicken browned and cooked through before the butter inside begins to seep out. The butter-penetrated white chicken flesh makes the dish delicious and rich, and there is a moment of surprise when you cut into it and the butter spurts out. Because the surprise is sometimes too great, restaurant chefs recommend puncturing the chicken breast with the point of a knife just before it is served.

KIEV CUTLETS

SERVINGS: 6

> *6 very small chicken breasts (breasts of 3 chickens)*
> *½ cup butter (1 stick)*
> *salt*
> *toothpicks or very small skewers*
> *2 eggs, beaten with a little salt*
> *½ cup bread crumbs*

Have the chicken breasts completely boned or boned except for the first wing joint and clavicle. The latter cut makes it possible to form the chicken breast, when stuffed, into the shape of a drumstick. In either case, it is important that the bones be removed with care so that there is a large, closed pocket for the stuffing. Nerves should also be removed.

An hour or more before starting the recipe, place half the butter in the freezing compartment. Preheat oven to 300° while preparing the chicken as follows.

Flatten the breasts with a heavy wooden mallet. Sprinkle them lightly with salt. Divide the ice-cold butter into 6 long, slender pieces and insert one into the pocket of each chicken breast. Tuck in the ends with

care and secure the openings with toothpicks or small
skewers. Dip the breasts in eggs beaten with a little salt,
then in bread crumbs. Repeat in the same order.

Heat half the remaining butter in a frying pan. Brown
the chicken breasts rapidly in very hot, but not burning,
butter. Add to butter as necessary. When all the breasts
are well browned, put them in an open casserole in a
300° oven until the chicken is cooked through. The
breasts should be small enough so that this will take
only 5 minutes.

Remove toothpicks and skewers. The chicken breasts
are good without sauce, but are usually served with
Mushroom Sauce (page 171).

CHICKEN BREASTS À LA MOSCOVITE

The Moscow version of stuffed chicken breasts, as
made at the Chicago restaurant Sasha's, is easy to prepare and delicious.

SERVINGS: 6

    ½ cup butter
    6 Tb pot cheese
    1½ tsp fresh dill or chives, minced
    6 small, whole boned chicken breasts (breasts of 3
        chickens)
    toothpicks or small skewers
    1 egg beaten with a little salt
    5–6 Tb dry bread crumbs

Preheat oven to 300°. Gently heat 6 Tb butter with pot
cheese and herbs while stirring until mixture forms a soft
paste. Stuff chicken breasts with this paste and secure
the openings with skewers or toothpicks. Dip chicken in

beaten egg and then bread crumbs. Fry it in remaining butter until well browned on all sides. Place browned chicken in an uncovered casserole without the addition of any juice and bake 30 minutes in a 300° oven. Remove toothpicks or skewers. Serve with White Dill Sauce (page 172). If sauce is thick, add a little juice from the baking of the chicken.

CHICKEN BREASTS "SOBKO"

At the Parisian restaurant Georges, this dish is called "Sobko" after the original owner, Sobchenko. It is a very festive dinner dish.

SERVINGS: 8

> ½ cup dark meat from drumsticks (1–2 drumsticks)
> 4–4½ oz. pâté de foie gras
> 1 Tb white wine or sherry or chicken bouillon
> 8 breasts of young chicken (breasts of 4 chickens)
>   with bones and nerves removed and a pocket left
>   for stuffing
> toothpicks or small skewers
> 2–3 Tb flour
> 2 eggs, beaten with a pinch of salt
> ½ cup bread crumbs
> 3–4 Tb butter
> 2 Tb olive oil

Remove meat from drumsticks and chop very fine; discard nerves, sinews, and skin. If the pâté contains truffles, chop those too. Mix chopped chicken meat with pâté. If mixture is stiff, thin it with 1 Tb white wine, sherry, or bouillon.

Dry the chicken breasts, stuff pockets with pâté mix-

ture, and secure openings with toothpicks or small
skewers. Dip breasts first in flour, then in beaten eggs,
and lastly in bread crumbs. Fry them, a few at a time,
in a mixture of butter and olive oil until browned on all
sides. As they are fried, remove them to an ovenproof
pan or baking dish. All the above can be done a few
hours in advance of dinner if more convenient.

To finish the dish, bake chicken breasts ½ hour in 300°
oven. They can be kept in a warm oven another 20–30
minutes without harm. Remove toothpicks or skewers
and serve with Mushroom Sauce (page 171).

POZHARSKY CUTLETS

Pozharsky Cutlets are named after the man who
invented them, an innkeeper in the town of Torzhok,
where travelers used to stop on the road from Moscow
to what is now Leningrad and feast on these cutlets. They
were originally made of partridge or other game, but
Russians make them of chicken today.

SERVINGS: 6 (12 cutlets)

    8 slices of fresh white bread
    1½ cups milk
    8 boned chicken breasts (breasts of 4 chickens)
    1 tsp salt
    ½ cup butter
    5–6 Tb dry bread crumbs

Cut crusts off bread, shred white part, and soak in milk
½–1 hour.

Set oven at 300°. Put chicken through meat grinder.
Squeeze bread to eliminate milk and mix bread with
chicken. Grind again. Mix in salt and 2 Tb melted

butter. With wet hands, form cutlets roughly in the shape of loin lamb chops. Coat them thoroughly with bread crumbs.

Fry chicken in 2 Tb butter, a few at a time, until browned on both sides. Add butter as needed while frying. Place browned cutlets in an ovenproof pan. When all are browned, put the pan in a 300° oven for about 5 minutes. Pour a little melted butter over the cutlets just before serving, or serve with Mushroom Sauce (page 171).

KAZAN PIE

Tartar Chicken Pie

SERVINGS: 10

DOUGH

1 cup warm milk
½ lb. lightly salted butter, warm enough to be soft
1¼ tsp salt
1¼ tsp sugar
1¼ tsp baking powder
3¼ cups all-purpose flour (approximately)

Pour warmed milk over butter, salt, and sugar. Mix baking powder with 3 cups flour and add to liquids. Add more flour if necessary to a dough that can be rolled easily. Mix just long enough to incorporate all the flour. Set dough aside, covered with a towel.

FILLING

1½ lbs. raw boned chicken (meat from 10 large drum-
* sticks)*
6–7 Tb butter
3 small onions, chopped
3 small potatoes, pared and cut into thin strips
* (julienne)*
salt and pepper to taste

Chop chicken. Heat butter and fry onion gently until
soft. Add potatoes and fry them until they are no longer
raw, but not yet browned. Add chicken and continue
frying. Use more butter if necessary. When chicken is
almost cooked through, season with salt and pepper,
remove the mixture from the fire, and let it cool while
rolling out dough.

BAKING

Set oven at 350°. Divide in 2 sections, the part for
the bottom slightly larger than that for the top. Roll it
out about ⅜″ thick. Grease a rectangular pan (10″ x
14″) with sides 1½″–2″ high. Sprinkle it with flour and
line it with the bottom part of the dough. Pour in the
chicken mixture, cover it with remaining dough, and
pinch sides together well. Make a few holes in the top
for the escape of steam, and bake 30–40 minutes or until
nicely browned.

SERVING

To serve Tartar style, make a chicken bouillon with the
bones and a little other chicken meat (or substitute 2
cans of chicken broth). When pie is baked, cut it in
sections and place each in a shallow bowl. Pour bouillon
over chicken pie until pie is almost covered. It is necessary to have enough bouillon on hand so that more can

be added as the pie absorbs it. A salad is all that is
served with it.

CHICKEN TABACA

Georgian Fried Chicken

SERVINGS: 3–4

    1 young chicken (2–2½ lbs.)
    salt and ground black pepper to taste
    3–4 Tb butter

Break the bones of the chicken so that it lies flat, but
do not remove the bones. Rub it thoroughly with salt
and black pepper. Heat a frying pan with 3 Tb butter
and put the chicken in it; it should lie in one even layer,
looking like this:

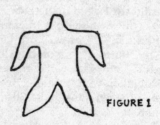

FIGURE 1

Add butter during cooking as needed.

Put a lid over the chicken that covers it but does not
rest on the sides of the frying pan. All the weight of the
cover should fall on the chicken. Put a heavy weight
(5–10 lbs.) on top of the lid.

Cook chicken over a medium fire about 15 minutes.
It should be browned; lower the fire for 5–10 minutes
and continue cooking chicken on the same side. Then

turn chicken over and cover it again with the lid and the
weight. Again, cook it 15 minutes over medium heat and
5–10 minutes over a lowered fire. It is done when all
moisture is gone and the chicken is delicately browned
and very tender.

CHICKEN ON A SPIT

SERVINGS: 3–4

> *1 broiling chicken (2–2½ lbs.)*
> *salt and pepper*
> *⅓–½ cup sour cream*
> *1 lemon or narsharab (pomegranate syrup)*

Split cleaned chicken in half, rub with salt and pepper,
and coat liberally with sour cream. Put on spit and broil,
turning frequently, until done (about ¾ hour). Baste
with juices and additional sour cream while broiling.
Serve chicken with lemon wedges or narsharab.

CHICKEN BOZARTMA

Azerbaidzhani Chicken Fricassee

SERVINGS: 4

> 1 young chicken, cut in 8 parts
> 2 medium onions, minced
> 2–3 Tb butter
> ½ bunch carrots
> 1½ cups meat stock, or beef bouillon
> salt to taste
> a generous pinch of cayenne pepper
> a pinch of saffron dissolved in ¼ cup hot water
> 2 Tb chopped parsley, mint, or dill
> ½ lemon, sliced

Wash and dry chicken and brown lightly with onions in 2 Tb butter, adding more butter as needed. Add carrots cut in straws; stir over heat for 2 minutes. Pour in hot stock or bouillon, season with salt and cayenne pepper, cover, and cook on low fire until chicken is tender (about 45 minutes).

When chicken is done, dissolve saffron in ¼ cup hot water and strain over chicken. Stir, check seasoning, and serve with chopped fresh herbs and slices of lemon on top.

NOTE: This dish is good made a day in advance and reheated, with herbs and lemon slices added only just before serving.

CHAPTER TEN

MEAT

LIKE fish, meat is often served with sour cream or sharp sauces of mustard and horseradish. Probably the most famous recipe for meat with sour cream is Beef Stroganov, a delicate dish named after Count Paul Stroganov, who was known for his gourmandise even at Tsar Alexander III's gourmet court. Less famous, but equally good are the veal and sour-cream skoblianky. Another aristocratic dish is shashlik, which, in its multiple forms, heads the following chapter.

There are roast meats, boiled meats, long-baking stews, quick-frying meat balls, and stuffed foods from meat roulades to roast suckling pig. The Caucasus and Central Asia have invented dozens of ways of stuffing vegetables and excel in meat and vegetable casseroles. There are raw meats, too: the familiar Tartar beefsteak and the less familiar Chee Keufta of Armenia. Despite the name, Tartars do not eat Tartar Beefsteak. A Russian restaurateur told me it was so named because the Tartar horsemen used to carry their supply of raw meat under their saddles.

SHASHLIK

Shashlik is a splendid dish for entertaining. It is as easy and quick to cook as steak, more decorative, and, like steak, can be broiled indoors or out. Like steaks, too, shashliks vary more in the cut and kind of meat than the preparation. Shashlik, or shish kebab, as it is known in the Middle East, are one and the same: pieces of meat roasted on a skewer.

This is an ancient dish throughout the Caucasus, Central Asia, and the Eastern Mediterranean. Homer described the grilling of meat over coals on skewers in the *Odyssey*. Probably no one can say with certainty whether it is originally Greek, Caucasian, or Central Asian, but shashlik is not a native Slavic dish, even though it appears on almost every Russian restaurant menu.

In the countries where shashlik has been made for the past thirty centuries or more, it is almost invariably made with lamb—preferably a young and tender lamb. In the Caucasus and Central Asia, beef is considered a substitute and a secondary choice. Nevertheless, shashlik can be made of pork, chicken, kidneys, fish, or of a combination of meats, as Ukrainians prefer.

Ideally, the meat should be grilled over evenly glowing wood embers. Ideally, but not necessarily. It is excellent grilled under a gas or electric broiler (although it loses the flavor of wood smoke); it can even be cooked in a casserole on top of the stove or in the oven. Recipes for shashlik in a casserole descend from an ancient herds-men's way of cooking whole, newly slaughtered lamb. The lamb was cut in pieces, salted, and tied up in the lambskin (wool side out). The skin was lowered into a pit in the ground and covered lightly with earth over which a large fire was built. When the fire died down, the lamb was ready.

The title of the shashlik usually indicated the cut of meat used. Karsky Shashlik, the king of them all, is made of large chunks of saddle lamb with the kidneys. Shashlik lyubitelsky calls for lamb ribs and Lyulya Kebab for ground lamb, while the usual shashlik is made of meat cut from the hind leg. The size of the chunks of meat varies: the Georgians like them so large that two or three take up an entire long skewer, while the Azerbaidzhanis cut them "bird-head size."

Controversy rages over the subject of marinades: whether to marinate or not, and if so, with what. Every cook seems to have adopted a theory and a favorite brew; one Russian woman told me her choice of marinade is champagne! My own theory is that the marinade was devised for two distinct purposes and should be used only to serve one or the other of them. One purpose was to preserve. Before the days of cold storage, marinades made it possible to keep raw young lamb left over from a feast-day slaughter for several days. The second purpose was to tenderize. When no young lamb was available and the shashlik hal to be made from an older, tougher animal (or even from mutton), the marinade made it tender and took away some of the strong flavor. In countries where shashlik is a native dish, marinades are not used on fresh, tender young lamb.

For classic shashlik, meat from the hind leg is cut in chunks and either strung directly on skewers or first kept in a cool place for an hour or so, sprinkled with ground pepper, onion, and parsley. In the North Caucasus, a little chopped garlic might also be put on the meat. For older lamb or lamb from the shoulder, lemon juice or pomegranate juice is added to the onion, pepper, and parsley to make a marinade, and the meat is left in it from four hours to several days. Both lemon and pomegranate juice preserve and tenderize meat, but both also remove some of its flavor.

Shashlik does not have to be served with rice. It is often accompanied only by small tomatoes or onions grilled on separate spears, or by a garnish of raw vegetables: strips of spring onion, rings of yellow onion, wedges of lemon, or sliced cucumbers. Sometimes the accompanying onion is flavored with cumin, a seasoning of which the Uzbeks are particularly fond. In Kazakhstan, the onion might be marinated in vinegar and sugar, and in Azerbaidzhan, in pomegranate juice (both marinades mellow the onion flavor). In addition, the grilled meat may be sprinkled on serving with minced onion and chopped parsley or other fresh herbs, particularly coriander.

Various seasonings are used with the meat. Azerbaidzhanis are fond of a kind of sauce made of kizil berries (Cornelian cherries). They share with the Georgians a taste for dried, powdered barberry, which can be obtained from Near Eastern groceries under the name of barberis or sumakh. This has a delicious tart flavor that can turn the most ordinary lamb patty into an exotic dish. Another good tart sauce for lamb is pomegranate syrup, known as narsharab, and a sweeter sauce is bekmes, or grape syrup. Both of these can also be found in Near Eastern groceries.

SHASHLIK OF YOUNG LAMB

SERVINGS: 6

> 3–4 lbs. lamb cut from leg
> ½ large onion, cut in rings
> a generous sprinkling of ground black pepper
> a bunch of parsley

GARNISH:

> 2 doz. tiny white onions
> 2 doz. tiny tomatoes

Cut lamb in large chunks, 1½″–2″ square, mix with onion rings, black pepper, and parsley in a glass or earthenware bowl, and leave it, covered, in the refrigerator for 1 hour.

Peel onions and cook them in boiling salt water until half done. Wash and dry tomatoes. String the vegetables on separate spears, or alternate tomatoes and onions.

Alternating fatty and lean pieces, thread lamb on long skewers and bring to room temperature before broiling.

Turn frequently to ensure even browning. Broil from
7–15 minutes or until lamb is cooked through. A few
minutes before lamb is done, put spears of onions and
tomatoes to broil. Bring them all to the table on the
skewers on a large platter.

GEORGIAN SHASHLIK

In Georgia, shashlik is not made the same way in
restaurants and private houses. For the former, an
inferior meat (shoulder, for example) is cut up in stew-
size pieces, marinated 3–4 hours in salt, pepper, chopped
onions, and peanut oil, and then grilled. The following
is the more elegant version, for home entertaining. For
this, you will need very long skewers and quantities of
fillet.

SERVINGS: 6

> 4–5 lbs. fillet of lamb, beef, veal, or pork
> 18 tiny tomatoes
> salt, pepper, and powdered, dried barberry (if avail-
>   able)
> GARNISH: 1 large raw onion, sliced, and 6 servings of
>   cooked rice

Cut fillet across the grain in pieces approximately 5½″
long and 1½″ wide. Alternate pieces of fillet with small
tomatoes on very long skewers. Grill over glowing coals
or under broiler 7–15 minutes or until done. Turn frequently during cooking.

On serving, sprinkle with salt, pepper, and powdered
barberry. Put 1 skewer of meat in the center of each
plate, and arrange raw onion slices on 1 side; cooked
rice on the other.

KARSKY SHASHLIK

SERVINGS: 6

>1 saddle of lamb with kidneys
>1 large onion
>3–4 Tb wine vinegar
>3–4 Tb dried tarragon
>salt and pepper to taste
>3 doz. tiny tomatoes
>2 bunches spring onions
>narsharab

Have the saddle of lamb cut into large pieces 2–3 per person. Grind 1 coarsely chopped onion in a blender or meat grinder, add wine vinegar, tarragon, salt, and pepper, and marinate meat in liquid ½–1 hour. Turn meat from time to time in the marinade.

Put 2–3 pieces on each of 6 skewers and broil lamb over glowing coals. Turn only once to brown on both sides. A few minutes before lamb is done, thread cleaned kidneys and tomatoes on separate spears and brown them quickly on all sides. Serve with chopped raw spring onions and narsharab.

UKRAINIAN SHASHLIK

Ukrainians are fond of combined meats, and even their shashlik calls for a variety.

SERVINGS: 6

> ½ *lb. lean salt pork or unsliced bacon (preferably*
> * smoked)*
> ½ *lb. fillet of beef*
> ½ *lb. fillet of veal*
> ½ *lb. fillet of pork*
> 6 *cleaned kidneys*
> *ground black pepper, sweet paprika, and salt to taste*

GARNISH: 1 bunch spring onions, each split in half,
                 lengthwise
                 2–3 lemon wedges per person
                 3–4 wedges of tomato per person

Cut meat in cubes of ¾"–1" thickness and thread them
on skewers, alternating kinds of meat. Sprinkle with
pepper and paprika, and grill in the usual manner (see
preceding recipes). Salt on serving. Garnish each plate
with onions and lemon and tomato welges.

UZBEK SHASHLIK

SERVINGS: 6

> 3 *lbs. lamb cut from leg or saddle*
> *ground pepper to taste*
> 1 *large onion, minced*
> *juice of 2 lemons*
> 1 *Tb ground coriander*
> *salt*

Cut lamb into 6–7 pieces per person. Sprinkle them
with ground pepper and put them in a glass or earthenware bowl with the onion, lemon juice, and coriander.
Stir. Weight the meat down, cover the bowl, and leave

it in the refrigerator 4 hours or longer. Salt just before cooking.

To cook, thread meat on skewers, 6–7 pieces per serving, alternating fatty and lean pieces. Turn skewers frequently while broiling, and broil 7–15 minutes, or until lamb is cooked through. Serve at once on the skewers with cucumber and tomato or other salad on the side.

LYULYA KEBAB

SERVINGS: 6

> 2½ lbs. ground lamb
> 2 medium onions, grated
> ¼ tsp cayenne pepper
> 1 tsp salt

GARNISH: minced fresh herbs and spring onions, split lengthwise, *or* sliced yellow onions and powdered dried barberry

The challenge in making Lyulya Kebab is to get the meat to stay on the skewer. The most effective method (but one to be undertaken with caution) is to have the skewers red hot when the meat is threaded on them. Put the skewers to heat first.

Mix lamb, grated onions, pepper, and salt. With hands dipped in hot water, press meat into long sausages, 2–3 per person. Taking great care to avoid burns, thread or clamp sausages on the hot skewers and put them over (or under) heat to broil immediately. Once the meat is seared, it will hold firmly to the skewer.

Serve sprinkled with minced herbs and onions or with powdered barberry and thinly sliced yellow onions.

CHEOP KEBAB

Here is a way of making shashlik without an outdoor grill or a broiler.

SERVINGS: 4

  1½–2 lbs. boneless, tender lamb
  2 medium eggplants (of the long, slender variety)
  2 Tb butter
  salt and pepper to taste
  2 large ripe tomatoes

Preheat oven to 350°. Cut lamb into 1″ cubes. Drop peeled eggplant into boiling salt water for 2 minutes. Drain, squeeze gently to remove excess water, and cut into 1″ cubes.

String cubes on skewers, alternating lamb with eggplant. Melt butter in frying pan or casserole and fry lamb and eggplant on skewers until light brown on all sides.

Arrange skewers side by side in a baking pan or casserole, sprinkle them with salt and pepper, and cover with thin slices of ripe tomato. Bake in a 350° oven for 30 minutes, or until both meat and eggplant are tender.

KAZAN KEBAB

This is a casserole shashlik from the old Tartar capital, Kazan, on the banks of the Volga.

SERVINGS: 6

> 3–3½ lbs. well-marbled lamb (or beef)
> 1 tsp salt
> 2 large onions
> 4 tsp powdered coriander
> 1 fresh chili pepper (optional)

Cut meat in pieces as if for stew. Sprinkle the pieces with salt. Slice onion in thin rings. Put a layer of meat, fat side down, in a casserole. Cover with a layer of onion rings and sprinkle with a little coriander. Continue, alternating meat, onion, and coriander. For a strong pepper flavor, add a chili pepper split lengthwise with seeds removed.

Cover casserole tightly and cook without stirring over low fire for 2 hours or until meat is tender.

BEEF STROGANOV

The following recipe makes the best Beef Stroganov I have ever eaten. I made one slight change in the recipe given me: the original called for 1½ lbs. of meat per person. You never regret having too much, I was told, particularly when it is so delicious reheated and served on toast the following day.

SERVINGS: 6

> 1 large onion
> 4–5 Tb butter
> 2 lbs. mushrooms, cleaned and chopped
> 1 heaping Tb flour
> 3 heaping Tb sour cream
> 2 lbs. well-marbled beef tenderloin (or tenderloin tip)
> salt to taste

The most important thing to remember in making Beef Stroganov is that all the ingredients must be at room temperature. Even the sour cream should be left outside the refrigerator for a few hours before the dish is started: it will not turn too sour no matter how hot the day.

Several hours before the dish is to be served, slice the onion very thin and fry it gently in 2 Tb butter. Fry the chopped mushrooms separately in 2 Tb butter. When both are soft, combine them, sprinkle them with flour, and mix well. When the mixture has cooled, gently stir in 3 heaping Tb sour cream. Let this mixture sit at least 2 hours; all afternoon if you prefer.

Approximately 1 hour before the dish is to be served, start cutting the meat. It will be worthwhile to have a well-sharpened knife ready because the cutting is the most time-consuming part of this dish. Cut the meat in thin strips lengthwise, then crosswise to make pieces 2"–3" long.

When the meat is cut and 20 minutes remain prior to the serving of the dish, put the sour cream-mushroom-onion mixture to heat gently over a pan of hot but not boiling water. While it reheats, fry the meat strips rapidly in 1 or more Tb butter. The butter should be hot, but not burning. Keep turning the meat with a spatula until it stops giving off juice (5–10 minutes). Remove it from the fire and allow it to cool for a few minutes before stirring it into the reheated sour cream-mushroom-onion combination. Add the juices from the pan and salt to taste. If the resulting mixture seems too thick, rinse out the pan in which the meat is cooked with 1 or 2 Tb water and add it. If there is not enough gravy (some mushrooms and meat give off more juice than others), allow the mixture to cool a little, stir in additional sour cream, and reheat the dish gently before serving. Serve hot with rice on the side.

VEAL SKOBLIANKA

Veal Skoblianka is a Beef Stroganov with veal; two versions follow. The first, in which the veal is cut in strips, is from the Russian restaurant Dominique in Paris. The second, in which the veal is cut in thin scallops, is from the Russian restaurant Sasha's in Chicago. Both are delicious, and both are quick to make. Sasha (of Sasha's claims his is a 7-minute dish. Serve them, like Beef Stroganov, with rice.

VEAL SKOBLIANKA (I)

SERVINGS: 4

1 small onion, minced
½ lb. mushrooms, cleaned and sliced
5 Tb butter
1½ lbs. veal steak
2 Tb flour
¾ tsp salt
¼ tsp ground white pepper
¾ cup sour cream, at room temperature

Fry minced onion gently with sliced mushrooms in 2 Tb butter until onions are lightly browned and mushrooms cooked through. Set aside.

Cut veal into thin strips, 2"–3" long, sprinkle them lightly with a little of the flour, and fry gently in 3 Tb butter until meat is tender. Toss frequently but carefully while cooking. When meat is done, add remaining flour, salt, and pepper. Blend over heat.

Remove meat from fire and wait until it is no longer hot (though still warm) before gradually stirring in sour cream. Return to low fire and continue stirring until sauce thickens. Add mushroom-onion mixture, heat to serving temperature, check seasoning, and serve.

VEAL SKOBLIANKA (II)

SERVINGS: 6

1 lb. fresh mushrooms
3 Tb butter
1 tsp flour
6 large, very thin veal scallops
salt and ground white pepper to taste
2 Tb sour cream

Wash, dry, and slice mushrooms. Fry them gently, covered, for 5 minutes in 1½ Tb hot butter. Mix in flour. Continue cooking gently for 1 minute, then remove mushrooms and sauce to another dish to cool.

Heat remaining butter in pan. Dry veal scallops, sprinkle both sides with salt and pepper and fry them over medium heat until cooked through (4–9 minutes, depending on the thickness of the veal). The scallops are done when the juice they give off turns from rose to yellow.

Stir sour cream into cooled mushroom sauce. Add salt and white pepper to taste, pour sauce over meat, and reheat dish gently to serving temperature without letting it boil.

CAUCASIAN LAMB SHOULDER

The following recipe comes from the northern steppes of the Caucasus.

SERVINGS: 6

> a 4-lb. lamb shoulder, cut in a square shape
> 1 qt. buttermilk
> 1 tsp caraway seed (whole or powdered)
> 1 tsp oregano
> ½ tsp rosemary
> 2 Tb fresh onion juice
> 1 clove garlic mashed with ½ tsp salt
> ¾ cup vegetable oil*
> 3 Tb sour cream
> ¼ tsp salt (or to taste)
> ⅛ tsp ground black pepper

Soak lamb in buttermilk for 24 hours. When ready to bake it, set oven to 325°. Mix herbs, onion juice, and garlic. Add oil. Gradually blend in sour cream. Season with salt and pepper.

Drain lamb. Put it bone side down in a baking dish and pour the seasoned mixture over it. Basting every ½ hour, roast in 325° oven for 3 hours.

ROAST SUCKLING PIG WITH KASHA DRESSING

Suckling pig is popular feast fare for Ukrainians, Lithuanians, Belorussians, and Estonians. It is a dish for the very rich—and for the very poor, as a Russian remarked to me: the first eat it because they like it and the second because they can't afford to feed it.

---

* Caucasians use sunflower seed oil.

SERVINGS: 12 (for a 10-lb. pig)

> 1 suckling pig (10 lbs. or less, dressed)
> salt and ground white pepper
> 1 recipe Kasha with Eggs and Onions, page 179
> 1 pig liver
> 1 large Bermuda onion, chopped
> ¾ cup chopped celery
> 2–3 Tb salad oil or butter
> 2 eggs
> ¼ tsp ground black pepper
> ½ tsp sugar
> 2 Tb parsley, minced
> ½ tsp baking powder
> ½ tsp rosemary
> paprika
> 1 potato
> cooking oil or butter or hot meat bouillon, for basting
> 1 polished apple

Wash pig with water, inside and out. Rub it well with salt, and sprinkle ground white pepper inside and out.

Preheat oven to 350°. Prepare kasha according to recipe on page 179. Chop pig liver and mix it with chopped onion and celery. Fry the mixture slowly in salad oil or butter. Add prepared kasha and raw eggs, ground black pepper, sugar, minced parsley, and baking powder. Mix thoroughly.

Stuff pig and sew it up. Put greased paper over the ears and tail to keep them from getting overdone. Sprinkle pig with ½ tsp rosemary and liberal amount of paprika. Place a potato in its mouth and bake it in a 350° oven until tender (a 10-lb. pig should be done in about 3 hours). Baste pig from time to time during roasting. For a soft crust, baste with hot meat bouillon or stock; for a crisp crust, with oil or butter.

Before serving, remove potato from pig's mouth and replace it with a polished apple.

NOTE: Kasha dressing is good with duck, chicken, or turkey. Add 1½ tsp poultry seasoning when using for fowl.

KARAJALAN UUNI PAISTI

Karelian Meat Bake

This is a long-baking stew from the far north, the Russo-Finnish border. It is usually served with boiled potatoes. Lamb or veal or both can be substituted for the beef, or all three meats can be used together.

SERVINGS: 8–10

> 2½ lbs. round of beef
> 2½ lbs. lean pork
> salt to taste
> 2 Tb peppercorns
> 1 Tb potato flour or cornstarch (optional)

Preheat oven to 300°. Cut meat in 2″–2½″ cubes, discarding fat from all meat except for ¼ lb. of pork. Starting with the beef, spread the meat in alternating layers in a casserole. Sprinkle salt over the meat and top it with the ¼ lb. of fatty pork.

Make 2 bags of cheesecloth for the peppercorns. Tie a long string to each bag so that it can be easily removed when the meat is done. Put a bag on either side of the casserole about halfway down. Press meat down firmly and cover it with cold water.

Bake in an open casserole in a 300° oven for 2½–3 hours. Remove casserole from oven and use a fork to separate the meat, which tends to stick together. Cover casserole, return it to oven, reduce heat to 275°, and bake

2–3 hours longer or until meat is tender. Remove pepper
bags before serving.

If desired, sauce may be thickened slightly. To thicken,
remove meat to a warm place, blend 1 Tb potato flour
or cornstarch with a little of the sauce, return the mixture
to the casserole, and cook, stirring, until it reaches
proper consistency.

BOILED MEAT

Russians often serve boiled meat. In the western part
of the country, where Ukrainians, Lithuanians, and Belorussians make soups with more than one kind, the main
course at dinner sometimes consists of several varieties
of boiled meat, cold or hot. The meat is usually left over
from the soup stock; here is a recipe for making boiled
meat independently and some suggestions for serving it.

SERVINGS: 6

> 3–4 lbs. meat for soup (brisket or round cut in a single
> piece looks attractive and can be evenly sliced; for
> taste, chuck is just as good)
> 1 bay leaf
> 6 peppercorns
> 1 carrot, cleaned and sliced
> 1 onion, sliced
> a bunch of fresh herbs (if available)
> salt

Put all ingredients except salt in water to cover. Bring
to a boil, skim once or twice, then reduce heat until liquid
is just simmering. Cover with a lid and cook until meat
is tender, but not falling apart. Add salt to taste about 1
hour before meat is done. Timing varies from 1½–3

hours, depending on the kind of meat and the size and shape of the cut.

Drain meat well and serve it in a single piece like a roast. It can be cut at the table or sliced in the kitchen and reassembled in its original shape. If meat is to be served cold, let it cool in the bouillon to prevent formation of a crust. Keep it wrapped and in the refrigerator after it cools.

Boiled meat, hot or cold, is best with a sharp sauce.

SAUCES FOR HOT BOILED MEAT

Prepared horseradish, prepared mustard, Hot Horseradish Sauce I and II (pages 173–174).

SAUCES FOR COLD BOILED MEAT

Prepared horseradish, prepared mustard, Cold Horseradish Sauce (page 174), Garlic-and-Yogurt Sauce (page 175).

LITHUANIAN ZRAZY

Stuffed Roulades of Beef

SERVINGS: 6

> 2 lbs. round steak cut in large, very thin slices and
>   flattened
> salt and pepper to taste
> 1 medium onion, minced
> 5 Tb butter
> ½ lb. mushrooms, finely chopped
> 2 large slices stale dark bread
> 1¼–2 cups meat stock or bouillon
> 3 heaping Tb mixed chopped fresh parsley and dill
> 2 Tb flour for dusting

Dry the flattened meat slices, sprinkle them with salt and pepper, and let stand 30 minutes.

Fry minced onion slowly until soft and golden in 3 Tb butter. Add finely chopped mushrooms. Continue frying gently, covered, until mushrooms are done (about 5 minutes). While they cook, grate the stale dark bread and heat the bouillon. When mushrooms are cooked through, stir in the grated bread, enough of the bouillon to make the stuffing moist (2–3 Tb), salt and pepper to taste, and chopped parsley and dill.

Distribute the farce evenly among the meat slices. Roll each slice in a tube, secure it with thread or butcher's string, and dust it lightly in flour. Heat 2 Tb butter in a casserole. Browning the ends of the meat roulades first in order to secure the stuffing, fry the rolls on all sides, slowly, covered, over a low flame. When they are lightly browned on all sides, pour in enough of the remaining stock or bouillon to almost cover the meat. It is best if the meat fits rather tightly in the dish so that no more than 1–1½ cups of bouillon will be needed. Cook gently, covered, 45 minutes; add bouillon if dish becomes dry. Stir frequently to prevent sticking as sauce thickens.

Before serving, remove threads from meat roulades and pour over them the sauce in which they cooked.

ZRAZY RUBLYONIYE

Roulades of Ground Meat

SERVINGS: 6

> 2 medium onions
> 4–6 Tb butter
> 1 lb. mushrooms
> 4 strips bacon, diced
> 3 Tb dry bread crumbs
> salt and ground pepper to taste
> 2½ lbs. ground beef
> 1 egg
> a few Tb beef bouillon (may not be needed)
> 2 Tb sour cream

Mince onions and fry them gently, covered, in 1 Tb butter while cleaning, drying, and mincing mushrooms. When onions are soft, put in mushrooms and cook, uncovered, until done; add 1 Tb butter if necessary. While mushrooms cook, fry diced bacon until crisp. Pour off grease and mix diced bacon with mushrooms, onions, and bread crumbs. Season to taste with salt and pepper and set aside.

Mix ground beef with egg and a little salt and pepper. Divide it in 6 parts. With wet hands, flatten each out in a rectangular shape about ¼″ thick. Place stuffing on each and roll it up in a tube.

Heat 2 Tb butter in a casserole. Brown meat rolls on all sides, then cover and simmer until meat is cooked through (about ½ hour). If there is little sauce in the casserole, add a few Tb beef bouillon to it. On serving, remove meat rolls to a platter. Stir a bit of sauce into 2 Tb sour cream. Add this, while stirring, to the sauce in the casserole. Pour it over meat rolls or serve it in a bowl on the side.

KOTLETY

Russian Meat Cutlets

Kotlety means "chops" or "cutlets." They are usually chopped or ground meat formed into the shape of a cutlet. In both appearance and flavor, they are far removed from hamburger.

KOTLETY (I)

SERVINGS: 4

½ *long white loaf of French or Italian bread, 1–2 days old*
1½–2 cups milk
1 lb. ground beef
½ *tsp salt*
a pinch of ground black pepper
2 eggs
2 Tb butter
2 Tb cooking oil
3 Tb sour cream at room temperature

Soak bread in milk to cover for 30 minutes. Squeeze hard to eliminate liquid. Mix bread with all ingredients except butter, cooking oil, and sour cream.

With wet hands, form mixture into flattened oval patties. Heat butter and oil in frying pan. Put meat cakes in pan when butter and oil are very hot; immediately reduce heat to medium. Without allowing meat to brown or form a crust, fry it on both sides, until it is cooked through.

Remove meat to warmed serving platter. Reduce heat. When pan juices have cooled slightly, stir in 3 Tb sour cream. Blend well, heat to serving temperature, pour over meat patties, and serve.

KOTLETY (II)

SERVINGS: 6

> ⅔ of the white part of a long loaf of Italian or French bread
> 3½ cups meat stock or bouillon
> 2 lbs. ground beef
> 2 egg yolks
> 2½ Tb melted butter
> 1 tsp salt
> a pinch of ground black pepper
> 2 egg whites
> 3–4 Tb butter
> 1 recipe Mushroom Sauce (page 171), or 2 Tb sour cream

Soak bread in 3 cups stock or bouillon for at least 1 hour. Squeeze it well. Add meat, egg yolks, melted butter, salt, pepper, and knead. Beat egg whites until stiff and fold into meat mixture. Form paste into shape of small cutlets or chops. Fry them gently in 2 Tb butter, adding butter as needed. As soon as cutlets are firm, but not yet browned, add remaining butter, remaining ½ cup stock or bouillon, cover the casserole, anud cook over low fire for 10 minutes.

Serve with Mushroom Sauce, or stir 2 Tb sour cream into pan juices and pour over the cutlets.

HARPUT KEUFTA

Armenian Stuffed Meat Balls

SERVINGS: 6 (12 large meat balls)

There are variations of this dish all through the Middle East. The Georgians make it flatter than the Armenians;

the Syrians make it flatter still. The Armenian name is
taken from the town of Harput in Armenia, where the
dish, or at least the Armenian version of it, presumably
originated. Once popular peasant fare, this unusual dish
is not quick to make, but can be almost entirely prepared
in advance. The interior of the Harput Keufta is like the
filling for Meat Beoregs, and can be used as is, cold for
an appetizer; Armenians who have lived in Arabic countries eat it that way, and it is delicious. The outside of
the Harput Keufta can be made into another cold appetizer, Chee Keufta (page 28). If you make a double
recipe of either stuffing or exterior, you will have a dish
ready for the following day with little additional effort.

KEUFTA STUFFING

1 lb. fatty lamb, ground (or ½ lb. beef, ½ lb. lamb)
2 Tb butter
1 cup minced onion
¼ cup minced green pepper
2 Tb chopped fresh parsley
1 Tb chopped fresh basil (or 1 tsp dried basil)
salt and pepper to taste

Fry ground meat in butter until half the moisture has
evaporated. Add minced onion and green pepper. Continue cooking for 10 minutes or until onion and pepper
are soft. Stir in remaining ingredients off fire and chill
before using.

EXTERIOR OF KEUFTA

*1 lb. very lean ground lamb (or ½ lb. lamb, ½ lb.
    beef)*
½ lb. fine cracked wheat #1
1½ tsp salt

For this dish to be successful, the meat must have no fat and be ground very fine. It is advisable to put it through the grinder 3 times.

Soak wheat for ½ hour in water approximately ½″ above level of wheat. Drain soaked wheat if excess water remains. Add ground meat and salt and knead. The wheat will expand as it cooks and require a little extra salt to be well seasoned; therefore, the mixture should taste slightly oversalted when raw.

FORMING AND STUFFING KEUFTA

Have ready a bowl of ice water in addition to the bowls of stuffing and meat and wheat mixture. Keep your hands wet and cool by dipping them in ice water from time to time while making the meat balls.

Place a lump of the meat and wheat mixture in the upturned palm of your left hand. The lump should be of a size that feels comfortable in the hand—perhaps about 1½″ in diameter. Shape the lump into a round ball. Now open the ball by inserting the thumb of your right hand. Leaving your thumb inside the hollow, rotate the ball in the palm of your left hand by tossing it very gently while turning it clockwise until you have a hollowed ball, about the size of a tennis ball, open at the top, and as thin as it can be made without falling apart. It is important to make the walls thin because they will thicken as the wheat swells in cooking.

Stuff the ball with the filling until it is about ⅔ full. Cup your right hand over the top and close the opening gradually, using your thumb and third finger. If the top is not evenly covered, add a bit of the meat and wheat mixture to close it and tamp the closing smooth with a little ice water. Smooth the entire outer surface with ice water. The ball is now ready to be cooked.

COOKING KEUFTA

8 *cups of any kind of stock or bouillon (chicken, beef,*
   lamb, etc.)
3 *Tb tomato paste*
salt to taste

Bring stock or bouillon to a boil with 2 Tb tomato paste.
Add enough salt to make broth just slightly salty. The salt
helps bind the ball together (cooked in plain, unsalted
water, it would fall apart).

Drop all 12 balls into the boiling broth and simmer
approximately 10 minutes. The balls will float on the
surface at first, then sink. When they rise to the surface
again, they are done.

Harput Keufta are usually served in deep, individual
dishes with a little broth spooned over them. Add 1 Tb
tomato paste to broth before pouring over the Harput
Keufta.

SINI KEUFTA

Broiled Armenian Stuffed Meat Balls

SERVINGS: 6–8

1 *recipe Harput Keufta (omitting stock and tomato*
   paste)
a little olive oil

Prepare stuffing, exterior, and make meat balls as described in recipe for Harput Keufta. Cut meat balls in
half and sprinkle oil on top. Put under hot broiler until
cooked through and browned.

TUKHUM DOLMA

Uzbek Stuffed Meat Balls

Tukhum Dolma makes a novel supper or luncheon dish, good with a salad or a green vegetable.

SERVINGS: 4–6

>   1 lb. lamb
>   1 medium onion, minced or grated
>   3 Tb fine, dry bread crumbs
>   ⅓ tsp salt
>   a pinch of ground black pepper
>   6 hard-boiled eggs
>   1 beaten egg
>   4 cups cooking oil for deep-frying

Grind meat fine. Mix it with onion, bread crumbs, salt, and pepper. Peel each hard-boiled egg and roll it in meat mixture until the egg is completely covered and looks like a round meat ball. Just before frying, dip meat ball in beaten egg. Drop in heated cooking oil and fry until brown. Avoid making the meat layer so thick or the frying oil so hot that the meat balls become dark brown before the meat is cooked through. Drain on absorbent paper and serve hot.

TAVA KEBAB

Azerbaidzhani Lamb Patties

SERVINGS: 4 (8 patties)

> 1 medium onion
> 1 lb. ground lamb
> ¼ tsp salt
> a pinch of cayenne pepper
> 2–3 Tb cooking oil
> 1 Tb wine vinegar
> 1 tsp sugar
> 3 eggs
> 2 Tb minced parsley (or mixture of fresh dill and coriander)

Preheat oven to 450°. Mince onion and combine half of it with meat, salt, and pepper. Form flat meat patties, 2½"–3" in diameter. Heat 2 Tb cooking oil and fry patties until brown on both sides.

Fry remaining onion separately in 1–2 tsp oil. When onion is soft and golden in color, add vinegar and sugar. Cook until liquid evaporates.

Beat 3 eggs with a pinch of salt. Stir the onion mixture and minced parsley into the eggs. Pour this over lamb patties and bake in 450° oven until eggs are just firm (about 3 minutes).

IZMIR KEUFTA

Lamb Patties in Tomato Sauce

SERVINGS: 6

>2 *lbs. ground lamb*
>2 *eggs, beaten*
>2 *cloves garlic, crushed*
>2 *Tb dry bread crumbs*
>*a pinch each of cinnamon, fenugreek, and coriander*
>1½ *tsp salt*
>¼ *tsp ground black pepper*
>2–3 *Tb butter, or a combination of butter and cooking oil*
>3 *ripe tomatoes, or 1 medium can tomatoes, chopped*
>1 *Tb water*

Mix the first 7 ingredients and shape into patties. Brown well on both sides in hot butter or butter and oil. Remove browned patties. Add chopped tomato and water to pan. Mash and cook over low heat until it forms a smooth sauce; add water if sauce is very thick. Return patties to pan and cook, covered, 10 minutes longer.

BADIMDZHAN MUSSAMBE

Azerbaidzhani Lamb-with-Eggplant Casserole

SERVINGS: 4–6

> 2 lbs. lamb
> 4 Tb butter
> 2 onions, minced
> 2 Tb lemon juice (or wine vinegar)
> a generous pinch of saffron
> 1½–2 cups hot water
> 1 bouillon cube
> 1 tsp dry herbs, or a sprig or 2 of fresh herbs (rose-
>   mary, basil, thyme)
> ⅛ tsp cinnamon
> a pinch of ground black pepper
> salt to taste
> 5 tender eggplants
> 1 clove garlic
> 2 Tb chopped fresh parsley

Cut meat in small pieces. Fry in 2 Tb hot butter in a
fairly large casserole. Sauté minced onion separately in
1 Tb butter. When meat is brown, add onion and stir
in 2 Tb lemon juice.

Steep saffron in 1½ cups hot water with 1 bouillon
cube. Strain into meat mixture. Add herbs, cinnamon,
pepper, and stir. Salt to taste and stir again. Cover
tightly. Simmer until meat is tender (30 minutes or
longer). Watch closely during cooking, adding more
water if necessary.

Peel eggplants, blanch by dropping in boiling salt
water for 1 minute, and then rinsing under cold water.
Cut into cubes, squeeze out excess moisture, and fry in 1
Tb butter. Add fried eggplant to meat. Crush garlic
clove and mix with meat. Check seasoning. Continue

cooking until eggplant is very tender (5–10 minutes). Sprinkle with chopped parsley just before serving.

NOTE: This dish can be made in advance and reheated very successfully. It is excellent with plain white rice.

RUSSIAN EGGPLANT CASSEROLE

SERVINGS: 6

>   2 medium eggplants
>   salt
>   2–3 Tb cooking oil
>   4 medium potatoes
>   1 large onion, chopped
>   2 lbs. ground beef
>   salt and pepper to taste
>   1 small can tomato sauce
>   catsup to taste
>   a bowl of sour cream

Slice eggplant in rounds ½″–¾″ thick, sprinkle with salt, and let stand ½ hour.

Squeeze out liquid and fry eggplant in skillet with a little of the cooking oil. Remove, drain, and set aside. Peel and slice potatoes into rounds of the same thickness as the eggplant. Fry potatoes in oil until brown. Remove, drain, and set aside. Fry onion slowly until transparent. Put in meat and continue frying until it is browned. Add oil as needed. Drain off oil and fat.

Fill a casserole with layers of potato, eggplant, and meat, in that order, repeating until all ingredients are used. Sprinkle salt and pepper lightly between layers. Season tomato sauce with catsup to taste and pour it on top. Cook, uncovered, on top of the stove over medium heat for 1 hour, or bake in 325° oven for the same amount of time.

Serve hot with sour cream.

LAMB-AND-LEEK STEW

SERVINGS: 6–8

> 3 lbs. boneless lamb cut from shoulder
> 1 Tb cooking oil
> 1 large onion, sliced
> 3–4 bunches spring onions, or 2 bunches leeks
> salt and pepper to taste
> 2 cups boiling water
> 2 egg yolks
> juice of 1 small lemon

Brown meat quickly over high heat in hot oil. When meat is browned, add sliced onion and the white part of spring onions or leeks, cleaned and cut in 2″ pieces. Sauté with meat for 5 minutes. Sprinkle with salt and pepper, pour in 2 cups boiling water (or enough to barely cover lamb), and cook over low heat 1½ hours or until meat is tender. Cook covered during first hour; continue uncovered if it seems necessary to reduce the amount of sauce.

Just before serving, correct seasoning and reduce flame as low as possible. Beat 2 egg yolks in a bowl with lemon juice. Add a little of the meat sauce to the mixture; blend well. Gradually stir contents of bowl into casserole. Do not allow sauce to boil after adding egg yolks. Serve at once.

NOTE: Lamb-and-Leek Stew can be prepared in advance to the point of the addition of egg yolks and lemon. The latter can then be added when the dish has been reheated and is about to be served.

AZHABSANDA

Steamed Lamb with Vegetables

SERVINGS: 6

>   3 potatoes, cubed
>   3–4 carrots, cut in straws (julienne)
>   3 tomatoes, cut in eights
>   2 onions, cut in rings
>   5–6 garlic cloves, peeled and whole
>   2 lbs. lamb sliced
>   2 Tb butter
>   2 green peppers, cut in thin rings
>   ½ bunch parsley (or fresh coriander), chopped
>   salt and pepper to taste

Azhabsanda is a steamed stew that requires 2 pots. One is filled with the food and left open. It is placed inside a larger pot containing water to a level of ¾ of the height of the smaller pot (as shown in the figure on page 23). The larger pot is tightly covered to prevent the escape of steam.

Fill the smaller pot with the ingredients in layers in the following order: potatoes, carrots, tomatoes, onion rings, garlic cloves, slices of meat, dabs of butter, green pepper, and parsley or coriander. Repeat the layers in the same order until all food has been placed in the pot. Sprinkle salt and pepper lightly between layers.

Simmer for 2 hours or longer: the more, the better. During the cooking, check to make certain that the water in the larger pot has not boiled out or boiled over, and that steam is not escaping. It may be advisable to weight the lid to prevent the escape of steam.

The juice is delicious and abundant, and the dish is best served in bowls.

MULGIKAPSAD

Estonian Pork with Sauerkraut

Mulgikapsad is a very popular dish all over Estonia.
Kapsad means cabbage and Mulgi is the name of the
Estonian province in which the recipe originated. A
delicious one-dish meal, it requires almost no preparation.

SERVINGS: 4

>   2 lbs. lean fresh pork in 1 piece
>   4½ cups sauerkraut
>   ¾ cup uncooked barley
>   1 bay leaf
>   salt and pepper to taste
>   boiling water

Put meat in heavy casserole. Cover it with sauerkraut.
Rinse barley in cold water and add with bay leaf, pepper,
and salt (put in little salt until the end in case the sauerkraut proves salty). Pour in boiling water until barley
is covered. Close lid tightly. Simmer over low flame until
meat is tender (1½–2 hours). Stir, correct seasoning,
and serve.

CAUCASIAN STUFFED PEPPERS

SERVINGS: 4 (4 stuffed peppers)

> 4 fairly small whole green sweet peppers
> ⅓ cup raw rice
> 1 onion
> 1 lb. ground fatty lamb
> ½ tsp salt
> ground black pepper or cayenne pepper to taste
> 2–3 Tb cooking oil
> ½ cup meat stock or bouillon

Cut off tops of peppers, wash and clean insides, remove seeds, and blanch peppers in boiling salt water. Rinse in cold water and drain.

Wash and blanch rice by dropping it in boiling water for 2 minutes, then rinsing it in cold water. Grate half the onion and add it to the meat with the rice. Season with salt and pepper.

Fill the green peppers with the stuffing. Heat oil and fry peppers, browning open side first to secure stuffing. Place fried peppers in a casserole, add stock or bouillon, and cook, covered, over fairly low heat for 15–25 minutes or until peppers are tender and rice is done.

Mince and fry remaining onion. Pour cooking juices over peppers and sprinkle them with fried onion.

HOLUBTSI

Ukrainian Stuffed Cabbage

SERVINGS: 6

> 1 large head white cabbage
> 1 large onion, chopped fine
> 2 Tb butter
> 1½ lbs. ground chuck
> 1½ cups cooked rice
> ground black pepper and salt to taste
> 1 cup tomato sauce (canned or homemade)
> 2 Tb sour cream
> ⅛ tsp sugar

Put a large pot of salt water to boil. Carefully peel off 3 doz. outer leaves from a head of cabbage (cut cabbage stem to make it easier to detach leaves whole). Pare the core of each stem to the same thickness as the leaf. Drop the leaves in the boiling water and cook until almost tender (about 5 minutes). Drain and put aside.

Preheat oven to 375°. Fry chopped onions gently in 1½ Tb butter until transparent. Add ground chuck and remaining butter. Fry until meat no longer gives off juice and almost all juice has been absorbed. Mix meat and onion with cooked rice. Season with salt and pepper.

Lay out cabbage leaves and put a heaping Tb of the mixture in the center of each. Fold the sides of the leaf over the filling, then fold down the stem, and, lastly, the tip of the leaf.

Mix the tomato sauce, sour cream, and sugar. Coat the bottom of a shallow casserole (about 2½″ high) with the mixture. Line the casserole with the stuffed cabbage leaves, face down. Pour more sauce over the top, cover the dish, and bake in a 375° oven until warmed through (20–30 minutes).

CAUCASIAN STUFFED VINE LEAVES

SERVINGS: 4 (20–25 stuffed leaves)

> 1¼ cups ground fatty lamb
> 1 medium small onion, either ground with the meat or
>   grated
> 4 tsp raw rice
> fresh herbs: about 4 Tb chopped parsley, dill, and
>   coriander (omit last 2 if not available)
> ⅛ tsp salt
> ground black or red pepper to taste
> 20–25 vine leaves, fresh or preserved
> 1½–2 qts. meat stock or bouillon

Mix all but the last 2 ingredients. Taste for seasoning: stuffing should be slightly peppery.

If using fresh vine leaves, drop them in boiling salt water for 2 minutes, then rinse under cold water. Preserved vine leaves should be rinsed in hot water. Remove stems.

Stuff leaves one by one as follows: lay the leaf down flat. Put 1 tsp stuffing in the lower center of the leaf (see Figure 1). Fold the 2 bottom portions of the leaf (1 and 2) over the stuffing; close the opening at the bottom as tightly as possible. Fold the next 2 portions (3 and 4)

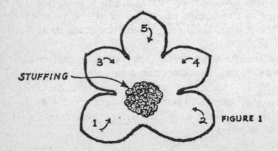

FIGURE 1

over the first. Fold the top leaf (5) down and place the vine leaf seam side downward until all are stuffed.

There are 2 methods of arranging vine leaves so that they do not unravel while cooking. The most common is to place them close enough to touch each other, seam side down in a casserole. Another method (which I prefer, and which makes removal of the leaves intact a simple matter) is to take ordinary cotton thread and a needle and string them like a necklace. In stringing them, take care to pierce the center so that the top leaf is caught and held in place by the thread. Tie the 2 ends of the thread together and drop the necklace into boiling stock or bouillon to cover. Put a lid over the pot and cook on a low fire 50–60 minutes. Serve with some of the sauce in which the leaves cooked.

NOTE: The Armenians like a dish of yogurt on the side; the Azerbaidzhanis prefer a Garlic-and-Yogurt Sauce (page 175).

CHAPTER ELEVEN

SAUCES

SOUR cream is a sauce in itself, the principal salad dressing in the north of Russia, and the basis for hot and cold sauces from mushroom to mustard. Northern Russians are fond of serving sauces spiced with mustard, horseradish or pickles on the side. Armenians, to the contrary, never use a separate sauce, but combine something—usually tomatoes or egg yolks blended with lemon—with the juice the fish, meat, or vegetable has produced in the cooking. Their neighbors, the Georgians, are famous for 2 sauces: walnut sauce, which they use on chicken, duck, vegetables, salads, potatoes, green vegetables, kidney beans—almost anything except dessert, and tkemali or tremali sauce, made from sour plums that grow only in Georgia and which American Georgians replace with rhubarb. North Caucasians and Central Asians like a little garlic crushed in meat bouillon to pour over meat dishes and dumplings, and the Azerbaidzhanis are fond of a cold sauce of crushed garlic in yogurt or sour milk, which they pour over stews. The last may not sound appetizing, but garlic enthusiasts will find it delicious with cold boiled or roast meat.

SOUR-CREAM SAUCE

SERVINGS: 2½ cups

>   2 Tb butter
>   2 Tb flour
>   2 cups hot meal stock, bouillon, or consommé
>   1 cup sour cream, preferably at room temperature
>   salt to taste

Melt butter over low fire. Stir in flour and cook slowly for 2 minutes while stirring. Do not allow mixture to brown.

Pour in hot stock or bouillon and blend well. Remove from stove to cool for a moment, then gradually stir hot mixture into sour cream. Return mixture to fire, reheat gently, season to taste with salt, and simmer for a few minutes while stirring until sauce thickens to gravy consistency.

NOTE: The same sauce is good with fish if made with fish stock instead of meat.

SOUR-CREAM SAUCE WITH ONIONS

SERVINGS: 2–2½ cups

>   1 minced onion
>   1–2 Tb butter
>   1 recipe Sour-Cream Sauce (above)

Fry onion gently in butter in covered pan until onion is tender. Add to Sour-Cream Sauce when final mixture is simmering.

MUSHROOM SAUCE

SERVINGS: 2–2½ cups

½ oz. dried mushrooms, soaked in ½ cup water
1 lb. onions
3 Tb butter
2 rounded Tb flour
1¾ cups boiling hot chicken consommé (for use with
    meat, substitute beef broth or beef consommé)
salt to taste
½ cup sour cream

Soak mushrooms in ½ cup water for 2–3 hours prior to starting dish. Reserve the water.

Slice onions and fry them gently, covered, in 2 Tb butter until they are golden and very soft. Sprinkle 2 rounded Tb flour over onions and continue frying while stirring for 1 minute. Slowly pour in boiling chicken consommé. Strain water in which dried mushrooms soaked and add it. Keep on low boil, stirrng occasionally.

Mince mushrooms and fry them gently in 1 Tb butter until soft. Add to sauce. Season to taste with salt and continue cooking until sauce is as thick as gravy. Remove from fire, allow to cool slightly, and stir in ½ cup sour cream. Reheat sauce gently to serving temperature without letting it boil.

WHITE DILL SAUCE

SERVINGS: 1½ cups

> 6 Tb sour cream
> 2 generous Tb chopped fresh dill
> 1⅓ cups canned chicken consommé or chicken stock
> 3 Tb cornstarch dissolved in a little cold water
> salt to taste

Heat sour cream gently until it melts. Add dill and
consommé or chicken stock; mix well. Dissolve cornstarch in a little cold water and add to sauce. Continue
to heat and to stir until the mixture thickens, but do not
allow it to boil. When it is thick, season it with salt to
taste.

HOT-MUSTARD AND SOUR-CREAM SAUCE

This is a creamy, rich sauce with a bit of sharpness,
delicious with roast meats or poached fish.

SERVINGS: 1–1½ cups

> 4 tsp butter
> 4 tsp flour
> 1 cup sour cream
> 2 eggs
> ¼ tsp salt
> 2 tsp prepared hot mustard

Melt butter. Add flour and blend over heat. Beat sour
cream with eggs. Stir in salt and sour-cream mixture.
Continue cooking while stirring until sauce is very hot,

but do not let it boil. Remove from fire, blend in mustard, and serve.

SOUR-CREAM PAN GRAVY

Russians use sour cream to make pan gravy from fried meats such as meat balls. Simply remove meat, spoon off excess grease, if any, stir in sour cream with pan off fire, and blend cream with all meat scrapings and juice. Season with salt and pepper, reheat, let it give one boil, remove from fire and pour over meat.

HOT HORSERADISH SAUCE

Horseradish sauce is excellent on boiled beef, cube steaks, and any other plainly cooked meat. It can be as sharp or as mild as you wish according to the amount of horseradish added. In the following recipes, instant or dried is preferable to prepared horseradish because the latter contains vinegar.

HOT HORSERADISH SAUCE (I)

This is a sharp sauce, to be used sparingly.

SERVINGS: about 1 cup

> 6 Tb instant (or dried) horseradish diluted according
>   to directions on bottle
> ¾ cup sour cream
> 2 egg yolks

Beat horseradish and sour cream together while heating slowly to a boil. When mixture boils, remove from stove and beat in egg yolks, one at a time.

HOT HORSERADISH SAUCE (II)

The following version is milder than the preceding one. Use it with cooked meats that need to be moistened by a sauce as well as seasoned by it.

SERVINGS: 1¼ cups

> 2 Tb butter
> 2 Tb flour
> 4 Tb instant (or dried) horseradish, diluted according
>   to directions on bottle
> 1½ cups beef bouillon or stock

Melt butter and stir in flour over low fire. Cook butter and flour together while stirring for 1–2 minutes. Blend in horseradish and bouillon. Continue to stir over heat until sauce thickens.

NOTE: Hot horseradish sauce made with fish stock instead of beef is sometimes served on fish.

COLD HORSERADISH SAUCE

SERVINGS: about 1 cup

> 3 Tb instant (or dried) horseradish (undiluted)
> ½ cup water
> 1 tsp sugar
> 1 Tb vinegar
> 6 Tb sour cream

Stir first 4 ingredients together and let stand 10 minutes. Mix in sour cream. Serve chilled.

GARLIC-AND-YOGURT SAUCE

In the North Caucasus and Azerbaidzhan, this sauce is used with cold roast or boiled meats, stews, and stuffed vine leaves. The amount of garlic can be varied to taste.

SERVINGS: ½ cup sauce

   3–4 garlic cloves
   ½ cup yogurt or thick sour milk

Crush garlic cloves. Mix with yogurt or sour milk. Cover and chill in refrigerator 4–5 hours before serving.

SASHA'S DRESSING

SERVINGS: 1 cup

   ½ cup mayonnaise
   ½ cup sour cream
   4 drops Tabasco sauce
   2 Tb minced dill pickle
   2 tsp red caviar
   1 chopped hard-boiled egg
   white pepper to taste
   salt (if needed)

Mix all ingredients, adding salt last and only after tasting; if the red caviar is salty, you may not need to add.

SOUR-CREAM DRESSING

SERVINGS: ⅔ cup

> *yolks of 2 hard-boiled eggs*
> *½ tsp salt*
> *½ tsp sugar*
> *½ cup sour cream*
> *3 Tb wine vinegar*

Mash egg yolks until smooth with salt and sugar. Stir in sour cream and vinegar.

BELORUSSIAN SWEET-AND-SOUR DRESSING

Belorussians like this dressing on salads of young spring greens such as beet tops and early lettuce because it does not overpower their delicate flavor.

SERVINGS: about ¾ cup

> *6 Tb wine vinegar*
> *6 Tb water*
> *2 Tb sugar*
> *½ tsp salt*

Mix until sugar has dissolved and toss young salad greens in dressing.

CHAPTER TWELVE

KASHA, RICE AND WHEAT
PILAFS, AND BREADS

KASHA is any baked or braised cereal whether it is buck-wheat, barley, pearl barley, millet, cracked wheat, oatmeal, semolina, rice, or even sago (palm pith). Buck-wheat is the most popular in Russia—rich, filling, with a nutlike flavor. Buckwheat is what is packaged and sold as kasha in America and it is what a Russian usually means when he says "kasha" without specifying the kind.

A staple of the north, kasha is used as a side dish in the same way as rice or potatoes. It also serves to stuff fish, fowl, meats like ribs or shoulder, and suckling pig (page 144), and can be made into a flaming dessert called kasha gurev.

Kasha is an acquired taste, but once acquired, liking quickly grows into recurrent longing. Different methods of cooking kasha are presented in this chapter in two recipes, one flavored with mushrooms and onions, the other with eggs and onions.

In the Caucasus and Central Asia, pilafs supplant the kasha of the north. In the mountainous parts of the Caucasus, the pilaf is of cracked wheat, sometimes called "mountain pilaf" because it is popular in the highlands where rice will not grow. As you move east toward and across the Caspian Sea into Central Asia, rice replaces other grains and gradually comes to dominate the menu

177

as a main dish and the chief fare at banquets. Azerbaidzhan is the first country on the journey east in which rice pilaf is a principal dish.

Throughout these countries, the way of preparing rice is a carefully studied and traditional rite; each has its own rices and its own technique for cooking them so that the grains are dry and separate. The pilaf, known in some areas as plov or pilau, can be made with meat, fish, vegetables, fruits, eggs, or even just an herb, such as dill.

In Azerbaidzhani pilafs, the rice and other ingredients are often cooked apart first, then together. The rice is washed and half cooked in a large quantity of boiling salt water. After straining, half the rice is sprinkled over a kazmag (flat, unleavened bread), lining a large casserole. The main ingredient of the pilaf—chicken or lamb which has been cooked separately until tender—goes in next, followed by the rest of the rice. The casserole is tightly covered, and the rice cooked without the addition of any water over the lowest possible flame. Every 15 minutes, the lid is removed and the accumulated steam allowed to drip off. When there is no more steam, which may be only after three hours or more, the rice is ready.

In Uzbekistan, every man feels it necessary to learn to make a pilaf when he reaches maturity, and it is the men, for the most part, who prepare pilaf for weddings and special holidays. The preparation of the Uzbek pilaf is unusual. It almost always starts with a braised meat and vegetable mixture known as the zirvak. To make this, meat, onion, and carrot, each cut in a specific way, are browned, salted, and then simmered in half the water needed for the rice. When the meat is tender, the rice and remaining cold water are poured on top, without stirring. The pot is left uncovered over a high fire and the water boiled hard until it is all gone. Holes are then poked through the pilaf so that all the steam will rise. The pilaf is covered with a plate and the cooking continued over a low flame until the rice is done. It is seasoned and stirred only just before serving.

KASHA WITH MUSHROOMS AND ONIONS

SERVINGS: 6–8

> 2 cups buckwheat groats
> 8 cups boiling water
> 2 medium onions, chopped
> 6–7 Tb melted butter
> 1 lb. mushrooms, sliced
> salt to taste

Preheat oven to 300°. Throw buckwheat groats in boiling water and boil 6 minutes. Drain and rinse under cold water.

Fry chopped onions gently until transparent in 2 Tb butter. Add mushrooms and continue frying over low flame until mushrooms are soft (add butter if necessary).

Mix mushrooms, onions, and 4 Tb melted butter with cooked buckwheat groats and salt to taste. Cover pan tightly. Bake in 300° oven at least 45 minutes (you can leave it in a low oven up to 2 hours; it will only improve). NOTE: Leftover kasha is delicious fried in butter.

KASHA WITH EGGS AND ONIONS

SERVINGS: 6

> 1½ cups medium-size buckwheat groats
> 2 eggs
> 3 cups boiling water
> 1 tsp salt
> 1 onion, diced
> 4 Tb butter

Preheat oven to 350°. Put buckwheat in a shallow baking tin. Stir in the eggs (do not beat) until all the grains

are coated. Bake in oven set at 350°, but leave oven door
slightly ajar. Shake pan frequently while baking to keep
groats from sticking. After 20–25 minutes, or when all
grains are dry, transfer buckwheat to large saucepan.
Add boiling water and salt. Cover and cook over low
flame 10–15 minutes. Add a little more hot water if
necessary during cooking. The buckwheat is done when
it is tender, doubled in bulk, and has absorbed all the
water.

Fry the onion in hot butter until tender and browned.
Stir onion and butter into buckwheat.

WHEAT PILAF

SERVINGS: 6

>   2 Tb cooking oil
>   1½ cups cracked wheat #2 or #3 (medium to coarse)
>   1 medium onion, minced
>   1 tsp ground coriander
>   ½ tsp ground cumin
>   3 cups chicken bouillon, salted to taste

Preheat oven to 300°. Heat in a casserole. Fry wheat
with minced onion while stirring until onion is transparent and wheat lightly browned. Stir in spices and
bouillon. Cover, bring to a boil, reduce heat, and simmer
over low fire 15 minutes or until just cooked through.
Bake, uncovered, in a 300° oven 30 minutes or longer;
the pilaf is done when all grains are dry and separate.

KESHKA

A porridge rather than a pilaf, Keshka is guaranteed to warm and fortify anyone on a cold winter's night. People are either very fond of it or dislike it intensely. Made of cracked wheat, soaked and boiled and beaten with shredded boiled beef or chicken until the meat is indistinguishable from the wheat, it is eaten with hot browned butter and ground cumin seed. For those curious enough to experiment, here is the recipe.

SERVINGS: 6–8

> *1 cup coarse cracked wheat, soaked overnight in water*
> *1 lb. beef or chicken (or other meat)*
> *salt and pepper to taste*
> *¼ lb. butter*
> *2–3 Tb ground cumin seed*

After soaking wheat overnight, discard water and cook wheat slowly in fresh water to cover until it is quite soft. In a separate pot, cook the beef or chicken in water to cover until it is tender (at least 2 hours for beef). Remove meat, shred with fingers, and return it to the pot. Drain cooked wheat; add it to the meat. Stirring occasionally to prevent scorching, continue cooking until almost all the liquid has been absorbed. Then whip the mixture, preferably with an electric beater, until the meat is indistinguishable from the wheat. Season to taste with salt and pepper.

Brown ¼ lb. butter in a frying pan. Dish porridge into individual serving bowls, form a hollow in the center of each, and fill the hollow with the melted, browned butter. Sprinkle the porridge lightly with ground cumin seed and serve hot.

TOVUK PALOV

Uzbek Chicken Pilaf

SERVINGS: 4

>   1 young chicken, cut in 8 pieces
>   5 Tb butter
>   3–4 onions
>   1 bunch young carrots
>   3½–4 cups water
>   2 tsp salt
>   ⅛ tsp cayenne pepper
>   1¾ cups long grain unconverted rice

Wash and dry chicken. Fry gently in hot butter until brown in a large heavy-bottomed or earthenware casserole. Add onion cut in rings. When onion turns color, add carrots cut in straws (julienne). Stir frequently. When carrots are lightly browned, add 2 cups water, salt, and pepper. Stir. Bring to a slow boil, cover tightly, and simmer until chicken is tender (20–45 minutes). Watch carefully; add a little water if much evaporates.

Sprinkle washed rice over chicken and pour in 1½–2 cups water. Water should rise ½″ above surface of rice. Increase fire and boil hard, uncovered. Test for salt; add if necessary, but without stirring. When all water has been absorbed, gather rice together in center and poke holes through it in several places to allow water remaining on bottom to evaporate. Cover tightly. Cook over low heat until rice is done (about 25 minutes). Mix rice carefully on surface before removing. Arrange on platter with rice on bottom, chicken on top.

KAVIRMA PALOV

Uzbek Lamb Pilaf

SERVINGS: 4

> 5 Tb butter
> 1 lb. boneless lamb
> 1 large onion
> 1 bunch carrots
> 2 tsp salt
> 3½–4 cups water
> a generous pinch of saffron
> a pinch of cayenne pepper
> 1¾ cups long grain unconverted rice

Heat butter. When it is sizzling hot, add lamb cut in small pieces. When lamb is brown, add onion cut in thin slices. When onion is golden, add carrots cut in slender straws (julienne). Stir frequently until carrots brown. Add salt, 2 cups water, saffron, and pepper; stir. Cover and simmer 20–25 minutes or until meat seems almost tender when pierced with a fork.

Wash rice and sprinkle it over meat without stirring. Pour in 1½–2 additional cups water (the water level should be about ½″ above the rice). Increase heat and boil rice hard in open pot. Test for salt; add if necessary, but without stirring.

When water has evaporated, heap rice together carefully on the surface. Poke several holes through rice with a knife or spoon handle to allow any water remaining on the bottom to evaporate. Cover tightly, reduce fiame, and keep at a low boil for about 25 minutes or until rice is thoroughly cooked. Mix rice with care on surface before removing.

Arrange Kavirma Palov on platter with rice on bottom and meat mixture on top.

AZERBAIDZHANI DILL PILAF

SERVINGS: 4–6

> a large bunch of fresh dill
> 1 cup long grain unconverted rice
> boiling salt water
> 1 egg
> a pinch of salt
> ½ cup plus 1–2 Tb all-purpose flour
> 1 tsp cooking oil
> 4 Tb butter

Wash dill in cold water. Cook it 1 minute in boiling water in a covered pot. Rinse it in cold water, mince it, and set aside.

Wash rice thoroughly. Cook it in a large amount of boiling salt water until it is half done. While rice cooks, prepare the kazmag, a thin flat bread of egg, flour and salt. Beat the egg lightly with a pinch of salt, add ½ cup flour, blend well, and then add as much more flour as needed to make a dough that does not stick to the fingers. Roll out dough. Cut a thin bread to fit the bottom of the casserole in which the cooking of the rice will be completed (an earthenware or heavy-bottomed casserole is preferable).

Heat 1 tsp oil in casserole. Spread it over the bottom. Put in the uncooked bread and dot it with butter. Strain the half-cooked rice. Sprinkle half of it over the bread. Mix in the minced dill and add the remaining rice. Put a tight lid on top of the casserole, an asbestos pad under it, and cook it over the lowest possible heat until done (unless the fire is extremely low, the bread, or kazmag, will burn). Remove the lid and let the steam drip off every 15 minutes until steam no longer forms. After 2–3 hours or more, when there is no more steam, the rice is ready. Pour in remaining butter, melted, stir rice gently, adding salt if needed, and serve.

ARMENIAN BREAD

SERVINGS: 5 thin breads the size of a cookie sheet

> ½ tsp dried yeast
> 2 cups lukewarm water
> 5½ cups all-purpose flour (approximately)
> 1 tsp sugar
> 2 tsp salt

Dissolve yeast in a little of the warm water. Mix flour, sugar, and salt. Make a hole in the middle of the dry ingredients; pour in yeast mixture and remaining water. Knead thoroughly. The dough should be thick enough not to stick to the fingers, but not dry. Add a little flour or a little water if necessary. Form a ball, cover with a cloth, and leave in a warm place to rise for 3 hours.

When ready to bake, preheat oven to 350°. Divide dough into 5 parts and roll each one out into a very thin piece as large as your largest baking sheet. Bake on an ungreased sheet 25–35 minutes or until lightly browned and crisp. Stack bread on end until thoroughly cooled.

NOTE: If stored in a dry place, this bread will keep for weeks.

AZERBAIDZHANI FLAT BREADS

SERVINGS: 10 round breads

> 2½ cups all-purpose flour (approximately)
> ½ tsp salt
> ⅔ cup warm water

Sift flour. Dissolve salt in water. Gradually mix flour and water together until dough is fairly firm and does not stick to fingers (slightly more or slightly less than 2½ cups flour may be needed to achieve the right texture). Roll dough into a ball, cover it with a towel, and let it rest 15 minutes.

Divide dough into 10 portions. Heat an ungreased frying pan. Roll out 1 portion of dough in a thin circle the size of the pan and put it in the pan to brown. When the first side is done, turn the bread over. If necessary, weight it down with a plate or bowl while it browns on the second side. Continue rolling out circles of dough as you brown the breads.

Let the breads cool completely on a rack before stacking, and stack them on end. If they become soggy, dry them out in a low oven before serving.

ONION FLAT BREADS FROM UZBEKISTAN

SERVINGS: 10–12 round flat breads

>   2 onions, minced
>   6 Tb butter
>   1 tsp salt
>   ¾ cup warm water
>   3 cups all-purpose flour (approximately)

Fry minced onion slowly in 1 Tb butter until onion is transparent. Dissolve salt in water. Melt remaining butter and stir into water with fried onions, cooled to room temperature.

Sift flour and add by sprinkling over liquid while gradually incorporating it until the mixture no longer sticks to the fingers; a little more or a little less than 3 cups may be needed. Form dough into a ball and let it rest, covered with a towel, for ½ hour.

Take individual balls of dough, 1½"–2" in diameter. On a lightly floured surface, roll out thin circles the size of the frying pan (7"–9") in which the breads will be browned. Brown them on both sides in a hot, ungreased pan.

Stack cooked bread on end after drying on rack. A basket or porous container is preferable for storing the bread until it is used. Laid flat on a plate, it will become humid and limp; it can be restored by drying in a low oven.

CHAPTER THIRTEEN

VEGETABLES AND SALADS

IF you ask a Russian what vegetable he likes, he will probably reply that he never ate one. Pressed, he will admit he consumes quantities of potatoes (which he never considered a vegetable), eats cucumbers, particularly pickled cucumbers, at all times of the day, and is fond of stuffed cabbage. Lithuanians like a few pickled beets with their pancakes or dumplings, Belorussians are fond of beet greens, and all northern Russians eat sauerkraut in soups and stews or by itself.

Unlike Americans, Russians seldom serve a vegetable alone; the vegetable is cooked in the soup or stew or does not appear at all. Nor does salad immediately bring a vision of tossed green leaves to a Russian's mind—if he is from the north, he might more readily think of herring and potatoes vinaigrette. The Uzbeks do not even have a word for salad in their language. Armenians, on the other hand, are fond of salads and use many vegetables. Most of the recipes in this chapter come from Armenia and other parts of the Caucasus.

Simply boiling, draining, and serving a vegetable is something that never occurred to an Armenian. Vegetables are sauced, or, if it is at all possible, stuffed. Tomatoes, squashes, peppers, pumpkins, eggplant, vine leaves, cabbage leaves, potatoes, artichokes, onions, zucchini—all are stuffed. In neighboring Georgia, vege-

189

tables are often seasoned with walnut sauce, while in Azerbaidzhan, they are topped with eggs and minced herbs.

AZERBAIDZHANI EGGPLANT OMELET

SERVINGS: 2–4

> 1 tender eggplant
> a few pinches of salt
> 1 onion, minced
> 2 Tb cooking oil or butter
> 1 ripe tomato, peeled and chopped
> pepper and salt to taste
> 4 eggs
> 2 Tb chopped green parsley

Preheat oven to 450°. Peel eggplant, dice it, sprinkle it lightly with salt, and let it stand in a bowl for 5–10 minutes. When eggplant has given off a quantity of juice, squeeze it thoroughly and fry it with minced onion in hot oil or butter. When the onion is tender and golden, add a peeled, chopped tomato and continue to cook until tomato juice is absorbed. Season mixture with ground black pepper to taste, pour over it 4 eggs beaten with a pinch of salt, and put the pan in the oven to bake until eggs are just firm (about 5 minutes). Sprinkle with chopped parsley and serve at once.

SPINACH WITH EGGS, GEORGIAN STYLE

SERVINGS: 4–5

>2 packages chopped frozen spinach (or 2–3 lbs. fresh
>   spinach, cooked, drained, and chopped)
>3 Tb butter
>2 onions, minced
>1–2 Tb minced fresh herbs (parsley, dill, fresh cori-
>   ander)
>salt to taste
>4 eggs

Drain cooked spinach thoroughly. Put over very low
flame with 1 Tb butter in a covered casserole that can
double as a serving dish. Fry minced onions separately,
covered, in 2 Tb butter. When onions are soft, mix with
spinach, minced herbs, and salt to taste. Beat 2 of the eggs
lightly and mix with spinach. Beat remaining eggs and
pour them on top. Spread them evenly over the spinach
and poke holes in several places so that eggs penetrate
downward. Cover and continue cooking over a very low
fire 1–2 minutes. As soon as eggs are set, dish is ready.

SABZI PIEZ

Braised Carrot and Onion, Uzbek Style

SERVINGS: 4

> *1 bunch young carrots*
> *1 onion*
> *1 large ripe tomato or 2 Tb tomato purée*
> *2 Tb butter*
> *salt to taste*
> *a pinch of cayenne pepper*
> *chopped spring onion and fresh coriander or parsley*

Scrape carrots and cut in fine straws (julienne). Slice onion in thin rings. Peel tomato and chop fine.

Heat butter and fry onion rings until brown over hot fire. Add tomatoes or paste and let liquid evaporate. Stir in carrots, season with salt and pepper, and cook 2 minutes longer. Add water to cover carrots, put tight-fitting lid on pan, reduce flame, and cook slowly until carrots are thoroughly tender (15–30 minutes). Sprinkle with chopped spring onion and fresh herbs.

CABBAGGE IN WALNUT SAUCE, GEORGIAN STYLE

The recipe below is highly seasoned with garlic; those who like a more subtle garlic flavor should put in only the tip of 1 clove.

SERVINGS: 6–8

> 1 Chinese cabbage (2–2½ lbs.)
> a small amount of salt water
> 1 cup shelled walnuts
> ¼ tsp salt
> 1 large garlic clove
> a piece of fresh or dried chili pepper, or cayenne
>   pepper to taste
> 2 tsp coriander seed
> 1 Tb minced fresh dill and parsley
> 6–7 Tb wine vinegar
> 1 medium onion, chopped

Remove any spoiled or spotted outer leaves from cabbage. Cut cabbage in half and cook it, covered, at a low boil in a small amount of salt water until tender (15–20 minutes). Drain it well. When it has cooled, use hands to squeeze out all remaining water.

To make the sauce, pound walnuts to a paste with salt, garlic, chili pepper, and coriander seed. Add minced dill and parsley. Gradually blend in enough wine vinegar to make a thick sauce. Mix with cabbage and chopped onion. Chill thoroughly before serving.

ARMENIAN SPINACH OMELET

Armenians like everything stuffed, even omelets. Their spinach omelet looks like a golden crusted covered pie.

SERVINGS: 2–4

> 1 package frozen spinach (or 1–1½ lbs. fresh spinach),
>   cooked, well drained, and coarsely chopped
> 2 Tb melted butter
> salt to taste
> 4 eggs

Mix spinach with 1 Tb butter and salt to taste. Beat 2 eggs well. Pour eggs into ½ Tb sizzling butter in an omelet pan (9″ diameter is a good size). Keep shaking pan and poking fork through eggs from time to time to ensure even cooking. When eggs are browned on bottom and almost firm, cover them with the spinach in an even layer. Press it into the eggs, place a plate over the pan, and flip it upside down to remove the half-cooked omelet.

Add remaining butter to pan, heat it, and then add remaining eggs, well beaten. Cook them the same way as the first 2 eggs. When they begin to set, slide the half-cooked omelet over them, spinach side down. Continue frying gently 2–3 minutes or until eggs are well browned on second side. To remove, place a plate over frying pan and flip it upside down again.

STRING BEANS WITH EGGS, GEORGIAN STYLE

This dish, Georgians told me, is usually a first course. I feel it would be equally good served as a vegetable with a rather plain meat, such as a roast.

SERVINGS: 4–5

>2 lbs. string beans
>2 Tb butter
>salt and pepper to taste
>1 Tb minced fresh tarragon
>3 eggs

Break beans in 1"–2" pieces before cooking. Drop in boiling salt water. When tender, drain thoroughly and put in a casserole that can double as a serving dish. Mix in butter, salt, pepper, and tarragon. Cover and leave on low fire for a few minutes. Beat eggs lightly and pour over beans. Use a spoon to even out the layer of eggs and poke holes through beans here and there so that the eggs penetrate downward. Cover casserole and cook until eggs are set.

SAUERKRAUT, ESTONIAN STYLE

SERVINGS: 4

>1 large (1 lb. 11 oz.) can of sauerkraut
>2 cups beef bouillon or stock (approximately)
>1 Tb sugar
>1 Tb butter

Drain sauerkraut. Take by handfuls and squeeze out liquid. Do not rinse. Place squeezed sauerkraut in saucepan. Pour in beef bouillon or stock to cover. Put lid on saucepan and simmer 2 hours. Add sugar and butter, mix well, and simmer another hour.

MUSHROOMS WITH SALT PORK

The following is a Belorussian side dish to serve with meat.

SERVINGS: 4

> ¼ lb. lean salt pork
> 1–2 Tb butter
> 1 lb. mushrooms, sliced
> salt and ground black pepper to taste
> 1–2 Tb sour cream

Cube salt pork and fry until brown. Pour off half the grease and replace it with the same amount of butter. Fry cleaned, sliced mushrooms gently with salt pork and butter until mushrooms are soft and some of the juice has evaporated. Season to taste with pepper and salt (bear in mind that the pork is salty). Allow to cool slightly before stirring in sour cream. The amount of sour cream needed will vary according to the juiciness of the mushrooms.

GRILLED SKEWERED MUSHROOMS

This dish can be used as a first course or to accompany a meat shashlik.

SERVINGS: 6

> 2½ lbs. mushrooms (5–6 mushrooms per serving, each at least 2″ in diameter)
> 2 Tb melted butter
> 2 Tb flour
> ½ tsp salt
> 1 bunch spring onions

Wash mushrooms. Cut off and discard stems. Drop mushroom tops in boiling water for 1 minute. Drain, rinse in cold water, dry, and put on small skewers. Brush with melted butter. Sprinkle with flour mixed with salt. Grill slowly over glowing coals or under broiler. Turn from time to time until evenly browned. Serve topped with minced spring onions.

POTATO KUGELIS

Lithuanian potato pudding, or kugelis, was probably German in origin, but is now one of the favorite dishes of Lithuanians. As they make it, it is not a fluffy pudding with baking powder or beaten egg whites; it is a solid, crusty, browned pudding, warming and filling, and served liberally spread with thick sour cream.

Every Lithuanian woman has her own recipe for Potato Kugelis. There are as many Lithuanian recipes for this dish as there are American recipes for potato salad. Some use only potatoes, onions, and eggs. The evaporated milk in the version given below helps to keep the potatoes white.

Pork roast and Potato Kugelis make a good Lithuanian winter meal—or a good winter meal anywhere.

SERVINGS: 6

3–3½ lbs. potatoes
2 fairly large onions
½ cup evaporated milk
2 rounded Tb dry bread crumbs
1¼ tsp salt
ground black pepper to taste
4 eggs
bacon grease (or butter or margarine)
a bowl of sour cream

Preheat oven to 400°. Grate potatoes and onions. Skim off liquid with a large spoon. Stir in evaporated milk, bread crumbs, salt, and pepper. Beat in eggs, one by one. Grease a baking dish with bacon grease, pour in the pudding, and bake it in a 400° oven 1–1¼ hours or until pudding is well browned. Run knife around edge to loosen pudding, and unmold it on a platter.

Serve cut in squares with a bowl of sour cream on the side.

POTATO KUGELIS WITH BACON

SERVINGS: 6

Ingredients for Potato Kugelis (page 197)
5–6 slices bacon (or thin slices of lean salt pork)

Prepare pudding for baking as in the preceding recipe, but reduce salt by ½ tsp. Dice 5–6 slices of bacon or salt pork and fry them over medium heat until all pieces are crisp and browned. Add them to pudding before baking it.

NOTE: Lithuanians add the fat rendered as well as the bacon.

POTATO PANCAKES

Potato pancakes are good as a lunch dish with sour cream and applesauce and as a side dish with roasts. Lithuanians like them with a topping of diced bacon and minced green onion tips, fried together.

SERVINGS: 4–6

> 2 cups grated raw potatoes (well drained)
> 2 beaten eggs
> 1 tsp salt
> 1 heaping Tb flour
> a pinch of baking powder
> 1 onion, grated
> several Tb butter for frying pancakes

Mix all ingredients together thoroughly. Drop batter by spoonfuls onto generously greased hot skillet. Fry pancakes on both sides until brown.

POTATOES IN SOUR CREAM

One of the favorite northern Russian vegetable dishes is new potatoes in sour cream.

SERVINGS: 6

> 2–4 potatoes per person, depending on size
> ¾ cup sour cream
> salt
> 2–3 Tb chopped fresh dill (substitute parsley if dill is
>   unavailable)

Boil potatoes in jackets, peel while hot, and toss gently in casserole with sour cream and salt to taste. Reheat, but do not allow to boil. Sprinkle with freshly chopped dill on serving.

ESTONIAN FRUIT SALAD

This preserved fruit can be kept for months in a cool place. Estonians serve it with meat or use it in salads. It is very good mixed with fresh citrus fruits such as orange and grapefruit.

SERVINGS: 6–8 pint jars of fruit (each holding 2–4 servings)

5 apples
5 pears
2 cups plums
1 cup cherries
several clusters red currants
2 cups water
1½ cups sugar
2 cups wine vinegar

NOTE: Any seasonal fresh fruit may be substituted or added.

Wash all fruit. Peel and quarter apples and pears. Pierce plums and other smaller fruit with a toothpick. Sterilize jars and lids by keeping them in rapidly boiling water 3 minutes. Drain them well.

Combining shapes and colors, arrange fruit in jars. Boil water with sugar for 4 minutes. Add vinegar, cover, and boil 5 minutes longer. Let mixture cool, then pour over fruit in jars. Use crossed sticks or weights to prevent fruit from rising. Close jars and store in a cool place or in refrigerator. Fruit is ready for use in 48 hours.

BELORUSSIAN WILTED LETTUCE

SERVINGS: 4

 ½ lb. lean salt pork or bacon
 2 Tb wine vinegar (approximately)
 ¼–½ tsp sugar (to taste)
 1 large Bibb lettuce or enough other tender greens
   for 4

Dice salt pork or bacon extremely fine (a 4-bladed onion chopper will speed the task). The finer the bacon, the tastier the salad. Put diced bacon or salt pork in a cold frying pan and fry very gently without shortening until well browned. Just before serving, remove browned bits to drain on paper. Add to the fat rendered in the pan an equal quantity of wine vinegar. Stir in sugar to taste. Pour it over washed and dried salad greens, toss until well mixed, and top salad with browned bacon or pork bits.

NOTE: A sweet red wine can be substituted for the vinegar and sugar.

CHAPTER FOURTEEN

DESSERTS

RUSSIANS are fond of fruit in desserts. Because fresh fruit is not available most of the year, they often use fruit jam and jelly fillings in pastries, dumplings, and pancakes. Fruit sauces are poured over fritters, candies are made from jam berries dried in the oven and rolled in sugar, and there are jam and cream pies and many fruit ices, ice creams and sherbets. One of the most popular desserts is kissel, usually a purée of tart fruit thickened with potato starch and served with light cream.

Cottage cheese is another staple ingredient of Russian desserts. It is made into tarts, dumplings, fritters, and pies. The Russian Easter delicacy, Paskha, is familiar to anyone who has been invited to a Russian Easter supper. One of the best desserts of all is the rich Vatrushka, made of cream cheese with candied fruits and raisins.

Ukrainian cakes are often baked with honey, and you find honey of increasing importance in all pastries as you descend southward into the Caucasus and eastward into Central Asia. Middle Eastern pastry consists basically of flour, water, and oil with some sweetening or flavoring— nuts or honey or both. The intricacy and variety of ways they have found to combine these few ingredients is a tribute to their ingenuity and to the patience of the women who make the pastries. The Oriental pastries and sweets are made at home for special holidays.

Desserts on other days are generally not sweet. Fruit is the Armenians' favorite dessert. Georgians favor fruit, too, but sometimes serve Khadja Puri, a cheese pastry containing no sugar, and Azerbaidzhanis prefer something cold and tart, such as their yogurt Dovga.

KISSEL

Kissel is a pudding, usually of fruit juice and sugar, thickened with potato starch or cornstarch. There are 3 kinds: a very solid kissel that can be unmolded like a gelatin, a kissel of the consistency of a cream pudding, and a thin one, meant to be drunk. The most popular is the semi-solid variety, often served with a thin layer of cream on top. It is quickly prepared and extremely refreshing, especially when made with tart fruit and little sugar.

Kissel can be made from any fruit—fresh, frozen, canned, or packaged as juice or syrup. Because most packaged fruits contain sugar, you will normally not need to add any when using them. When it is traditional to use potato starch, cornstarch can be substituted; proportions for both are given in the following recipes.

RASPBERRY KISSEL MADE WITH FROZEN FRUIT

SERVINGS: 6

> 3 12-oz. packages of frozen raspberries packed in
> syrup
> 1 cup water
> sugar to taste
> 4½ tsp potato starch dissolved in ¼ cup water*
> ½ cup light cream (approximately)

Put raspberries and water in an enamel or brass pot,
bring to a slow boil, and simmer until berries are soft.
Watch with care: they can boil over rapidly.

Pass soft berries through a fine sieve; discard seeds.
Taste and add sugar if necessary, bearing in mind that
kissel should be tart, not sweet. Return pot to stove.

Dissolve potato starch in ¼ cup cold water and stir it
into the hot liquid with a wooden spoon. Bring mixture
to a boil, let it bubble once, and pour it into a shallow
dessert serving bowl or individual dishes. To prevent
the formation of a hard film on top, immediately cover
the kissel with a lid or aluminum foil. When the kissel
has reached room temperature, put it in the refrigerator
to chill. Serve cold with a thin layer of light cream.

KISSEL MADE WITH FRESH BERRIES

Kissel made with any kind of fresh berries is delicious:
blueberries, cherries, cranberries, currants, raspberries,
or strawberries.

---

* 2 Tb plus 2 tsp cornstarch may be substituted for potato
starch, and more or less of either starch may be used to make a
thicker or thinner kissel. If you are using cornstarch, boil liquid
until it becomes clear (1–2 minutes) after adding starch.

SERVINGS: 8

> *1½ lbs. berries*
> *6 cups cold water (including berry juices)*
> *sugar to taste*
> *potato starch or cornstarch*
> *½–¾ cup light cream*

Wash and clean berries. Crush or mash them. Save the juice, measure it, and add enough water to make 6 cups of liquid. Hold 1 cup in reserve. Bring the remaining 5 cups to a boil with the crushed berries. Simmer until berries are very soft. Strain and reheat liquid. Add sugar to taste.

To determine the amount of starch needed, measure liquid. Counting the cup held in reserve, use 1½ tsp potato starch per 1¼ cups liquid or 2 tsp cornstarch per cup. Dissolve starch in reserved juice; add it to the hot fruit syrup. If using potato starch, bring mixture to a boil and let it boil once before pouring into serving dishes. If using cornstarch, let liquid boil until it becomes clear (1–2 minutes). Cover immediately after pouring into serving dishes. Serve chilled, topped with light cream.

APPLE KISSEL

SERVINGS: 8

> *5–6 medium apples, washed, cored, and chopped*
> *6 cups water*
> *½ stick cinnamon*
> *sugar to taste*
> *cornstarch or potato starch dissolved in ¼ cup cold water*

Bring apples to a boil with water and cinnamon; simmer until apples are soft. Stir sugar to taste into liquid. Measure liquid and reheat it. Stir into ¼ cup cold water 1½ tsp potato starch for every 1¼ cups liquid or 2 tsp cornstarch for every cup. Continue as described in the preceding recipe. Serve with a little light cream on top if you like.

CRANBERRY JUICE KISSEL

With bottled fruit juices, kissel can be prepared in 2 minutes. Cranberry juice cocktail is the base of the following, but other bottled fruit juices and syrups combined with each other or thinned with water can be substituted. Sweeten the liquid with sugar or fruit jam until it has a blend of tartness and sweetness to your taste, measure the liquid to determine the amount of starch needed, and proceed as described in the recipe for Kissel Made with Fresh Berries on page 205.

SERVINGS: 6

> 3¾ cups bottled cranberry juice cocktail
> ¼ cup lemon juice
> 4 tsp sugar (or to taste)
> either 4½ tsp potato starch or 2 Tb plus 2 tsp corn-
> starch, dissolved in ¼ cup cold water
> ½ cup light cream (approximately)

Heat juices with sugar, add starch dissolved in cold water, let cornstarch boil until liquid clears, but only allow potato starch to bubble once before pouring into serving dish. Cover dish immediately and chill after it reaches room temperature. Serve with a little light cream on top.

VATRUSHKA

Vatrushka, often baked in the form of small individual pastries called vatrushky, is the Russian equivalent of cheese cake. Made according to the recipe below (from the Russian restaurant Georges, in Paris), it is more than an equivalent: it is a superlative dessert.

SERVINGS: 8–10

PASTRY

1¼ cups sugar
4½ cups all-purpose flour
½ tsp salt
½ lb. lightly salted butter
3 eggs

Sift sugar, flour, and salt into large bowl. Add butter cut into bits. Mix with fingertips until butter is evenly distributed throughout flour. Add eggs and continue blending. Roll pastry into a ball, place it on a flat surface, and further blend it by alternately pushing on the mass with the heel of one hand and folding the dough over. When it is thoroughly blended, roll it out approximately ⅜″ thick on a very lightly floured surface.

Butter a large, circular layer cake pan with straight sides. Line the pan with a thick layer of dough; let the dough project above the sides of the pan to allow for contraction during baking. Set oven at 350° before starting filling.

FILLING

8 oz. cream cheese
7 Tb sugar
4 eggs
3 Tb vodka
3 Tb candied fruit*
1 heaping Tb seedless raisins

Beat cream cheese until smooth. Add sugar and mix well. Gradually blend in eggs and vodka. Stir fruit and raisins in by hand and pour filling into uncooked pastry shell. Distribute fruit and raisins as evenly as possible as you pour. Bake in 350° oven approximately 30 minutes (or until pastry is lightly browned and filling just firm).

If baking tin does not have a false bottom, unmold as follows when pastry has cooled. Place a large plate over pastry. With one hand under pastry pan and the other holding the plate, flip the pastry over onto the plate. Quickly put a second large plate against the underside of the pastry and flip it again to bring it right side up.

LEFTOVER-BLINY COFFEE CAKE

SERVINGS: 1 round coffee cake (9″ in diameter)

1 cup unsifted flour
½ cup sugar
½ recipe bliny batter from page 104
4–5 large green cooking apples
juice of ½ lemon
½ tsp cinnamon
½ tsp powdered ginger
4 Tb sugar
1 Tb butter

---

* Make certain that the fruit does not have a bitter taste.

Stir flour and sugar into batter with wooden spoon. Cover bowl with towel and leave in warm place for 1 hour or until it rises again.

Preheat oven to 400°. Core and pare apples, cut them in pie slices into a bowl containing lemon juice. Mix cinnamon, ginger, and sugar together and stir into apple slices.

Pour batter into greased baking tin lined with paper. Spread apples over top, pressing them lightly into the batter. Dot surface with butter and bake 30–35 minutes in a 400° oven. Cake is done when it is just firm to the touch and when a toothpick inserted in the middle comes out clean.

NOTE: The cake can be made with any fruit, canned, frozen, or fresh: blueberries, strawberries, cherries, etc. With fruit other than apples, omit cinnamon and ginger and add sugar in proportion to the sweetness of the fruit.

TARTAR APRICOT PIE

It seems surprising that apricot pie would be a favored dessert among the Tartars, but this is an authentic Tartar recipe for special occasions.

SERVINGS: 10–12

FILLING

1 lb. dried apricots, washed, cut in fairly large pieces, and soaked overnight in water to cover
2 cups sugar

Put apricots, their juice, and 2 cups sugar over a low fire. Stir frequently to prevent sticking and burning. When apricots are soft, set filling aside to cool.

DOUGH

½ lb. butter
¼ cup sugar
2 eggs
¾ cup sour cream
3¼–3½ cups flour
1¼ tsp salt
5 tsp single-action baking powder

TOPPING

2 Tb butter
3 Tb flour
2 tsp sugar

Preheat oven to 375°. Cream butter and sugar thoroughly. Gradually add 2 eggs, lightly beaten. Using a wooden spoon, mix in ¾ cup sour cream. Sift 3¼ cups flour with salt and baking powder, and blend in rapidly. The dough should have just enough flour to be easy to roll out. Add the ¼ cup flour held in reserve only if the dough still sticks to the fingers.

Butter a 9″ x 12″ baking tin with high sides (1¾″– 2″), and dust it lightly with flour. Divide dough in 2 parts, the one destined for the bottom larger than the top. Roll them out. Line the tin with the larger, pour in the cooled apricots, and place the second sheet of dough over the top. Pinch the edges together firmly.

Prepare topping by cutting the butter, flour, and sugar together with a pastry blender or blending them with fingertips. Sprinkle this mixture over pie crust, make 3–4 small holes in the top to allow the escape of steam, and bake the pie approximately 30 minutes in the top rack of a 375° oven.

UKRAINIAN POPPY-SEED CAKE

This cake is like a coffee cake, very good for breakfast or with a fruit dessert or an ice. Ukrainians take pride in grinding their own poppy seeds fresh for each occasion, but ground poppy seed also gives a very good flavor. It can be bought inexpensively in bulk at German and East European delicatessens.

SERVINGS: 1 loaf cake

> 1 cup ground poppy seed
> 1 cup milk
> 1 cup butter
> 2 cups sugar
> 3 eggs, separated
> 2 cups flour
> ½ tsp salt
> 2½ tsp double action baking powder
> 2 tsp vanilla extract
> powdered sugar

Put poppy seed in milk, bring to a boil, and set it aside for 1 hour.

Preheat oven to 350°. Cream butter and sugar together. Beat in egg yolks. Add poppy seed-milk mixture. Sift flour, salt, and baking powder; stir into dough. Beat whites of egg until stiff, and fold into dough with vanilla.

Grease a large loaf pan with butter or margarine. Sprinkle flour over sides, fill pan, and bake approximately 1 hour. If it springs back when touched with a finger and if a toothpick inserted in the middle comes out clean, the cake is ready. Invert it over a rack to cool. Just before serving, sprinkle powdered sugar on top.

NOTE: To make cupcakes from this dough, bake in buttered and floured muffin tins for about 25 minutes.

KHADJA PURI

In Georgia, Khadja Puri is a common dessert although it contains no sugar. It is basically cheese and bread, as its name indicates in Georgian (khadja = cheese and puri = bread). Serving it for dessert is perhaps no stranger than serving cheese and crackers, but I prefer it as a first course, where it is on a par with cheese soufflé and quiche Lorraine. The only danger in serving it first is the almost uncontrollable urge to eat more than is consistent with an "appetizer" or first course. Khadja Puri also makes an ideal late supper, a superior Georgian rarebit. Another departure from tradition I suggest to those who like to experiment is to try it with various kinds of cheese.

SERVINGS: 6–8

FILLING

1 lb. feta cheese
1 egg
1 Tb butter at room temperature

Feta cheese is preserved in salt brine; the longer it is kept in the brine, the saltier it is. In Georgia, fresh feta cheese does not need to be soaked for desalting, but cheese sold in the U.S. will be salty to varying degrees. To desalt, cut cheese in small pieces, put them in a china or earthenware bowl, and pour in cold water to cover cheese liberally. Leave it 2–5 hours; the time depends on the degree of saltiness (taste to test). When cheese is no longer salty, drain it thoroughly in a sieve. Then force it through the sieve and mix it with raw egg and 1 Tb butter.

DOUGH

3 cups all-purpose flour
1 tsp sugar
½ tsp salt
2 Tb butter at room temperature
1 cup milk
1 egg, lightly beaten
1 egg white, beaten to blend

Sift flour with sugar and salt into bowl or onto pastry slab. Make a hollow in the middle of the heap of flour and put in the butter, milk, and lightly beaten egg. Mix with fingers until well blended, then form 2 balls of dough. Roll each out in a thin circle twice the size of the frying pan to be used for browning the Khadja Puri (a 9″ or 10″ pan will serve very well).

Divide cheese filling in 2 equal parts. On each round of dough, spread an even layer of the cheese mixture in an inner circle the size of the frying pan. A large border will be left uncovered by filling. Pleat the eggs of the border in such a way as to close the border entirely over the filling. Pinch the edges together firmly and seal them with white of egg.

FRYING

2 Tb butter

Heat frying pan. When it is hot, drop in 1 Tb butter. As soon as butter melts, put in the first Khadja Puri, seam side down. Cover the pan and fry for a few minutes or until nicely browned on the bottom. Turn Khadja Puri over and brown the second side in an uncovered pan. Repeat process for the second Khadja Puri. Serve hot.

NOTE: Khadja Puri is never eaten cold. It can be cooked very rapidly at the last moment if both filling and dough have been prepared in advance.

PASKHA

Paskha, a special Russian cheese cake, is made at Easter and only at Easter. It is eaten with kulich, a kind of coffee cake, equally traditional at Easter. Some cake of this sort, whether it is stollen or baba or something similar, must be served with Paskha; it does not stand alone.

The recipe below is delicious and simple. The only hard part is the beating, for Paskha should be beaten until not a single lump remains. I have heard women boast that their Paskhas are beaten without stopping for several hours, or even all day. This is certainly an exaggeration, but because the dough is stiff and worked, traditionally, with a wooden spoon, it is best to make Paskha when there is someone around with whom to relay the beating.

SERVINGS: 12–15

3 lbs. pot cheese
1 lb. unsalted butter
3 well-beaten whole eggs
1 Tb vanilla extract
2 cups sugar
¼ cup seedless raisins
cheesecloth and a large, conical clay flowerpot with a
    hole in the bottom*

---

* The flowerpot is for the draining of the Paskha and the cheesecloth serves to line the pot. In Russia, a special wooden form, usually a tall triangle, is lined with a napkin to receive the moist Pashka. Russian-Americans use a flowerpot.

Put pot cheese and butter through a meat grinder together, using a regular grind. Do not use a blender, which will turn it into a purée. After grinding, mix thoroughly with a large wooden spoon until the mass is absolutely smooth.

Add 3 well-beaten eggs with 1 Tb vanilla and 2 cups of sugar. Beat it again, thoroughly, for 10–15 minutes. It should be entirely lump-free.

Wash and dry the flowerpot. Line it as smoothly as possible with several layers of cheesecloth. Pour in the Paskha mixture, cover the top with cheesecloth, and weight it down evenly with a heavy weight: a stone mortar, canned goods—whatever is handy and heavy. Put a flat plate under the weight if necessary to distribute it equally.

Place the Paskha in the refrigerator with a dish underneath to catch the liquid that will drain through the hole in the bottom of the flowerpot. Leave it there for 24 hours (longer if you wish: it will keep a week). After 24 hours, you will find the dish for the liquid full and the Paskha much reduced in size. This is as it should be: nothing is worse than a moist Paskha. Unwrap the cheesecloth from the top, hold a plate over the flowerpot and flip it upside down to unmold. Remove the cheesecloth and decorate the cake with raisins.

NOTE: The Russian initials (X.B.) for the traditional Easter greeting, "Christ is risen," are often etched on the side of the Paskha or outlined in raisins.

WALNUT CRESCENTS

SERVINGS: 2 dozen

¼ lb. lightly salted butter
2¾ cups all-purpose flour
½ tsp salt
2 tsp baking powder
½ cup milk
2 large eggs
2 Tb melted butter
1 egg yolk
1 tsp water
¾ cup sugar
¾ tsp cinnamon
2 Tb chopped golden seedless raisins or dried currants
4 heaping Tb ground walnuts

Have butter at room temperature. Using fingers, blend butter with flour, salt, and baking powder until the mixture is the consistency of fine cornmeal. Make a hole in the center, add milk beaten with 2 eggs, and blend thoroughly again. Divide the dough in 3 parts and form 3 balls with lightly floured hands. Cover with a cloth and refrigerate for 1 hour.

Because of its high butter content, the dough should be left in the refrigerator until it is to be rolled; otherwise it will become soft and hard to handle. Before removing the dough, heat oven to 375°. Have ready 2 Tb melted butter, a pastry brush, an egg yolk beaten with 1 tsp water for brushing pastry, and the filling. The filling consists of the sugar, cinnamon, raisins or currants, and ground walnuts, mixed. (Grind walnuts in a mortar or electric blender.)

Remove from the refrigerator only 1 ball of dough at a time. Prepare each one as follows. Roll out quickly on a lightly floured board in the shape of a large pie.

Cut the circle into 8 wedges like a pie, brush each wedge
lightly with melted butter, and sprinkle all but the very
center with filling. Roll up each wedge, starting with
the broad end and finishing with the point. Curve each
in the form of a crescent and place it, point side up, on
an ungreased baking sheet. When all the dough has
been rolled out, brush the tops with the egg yolk-water
mixture. Bake in a 375° oven for 25 minutes or until
crescents are browned on top and firm to the touch.

DOVGA

This is a dessert for those who share the Azerbaidzhanis' dislike for sweets after a meal.

SERVINGS: 4

> 1 pint yogurt
> ½ cup cooked rice
> 4 Tb chopped cooked spinach
> 3 Tb chopped fresh dill

Beat yogurt until it looks like buttermilk. Add rice. Heat
yogurt, beating it without stopping until it comes to a
boil; once yogurt boils, it ceases to be in danger of
curdling. Stir in spinach and dill and serve.

NOTE: Dovga can also be made with raw rice and raw
spinach. In that case, reduce the amount of rice, increase
the amount of spinach, and cook 15–20 minutes after
yogurt boils or until rice and spinach are done.

HALVA

Halva is a kind of candy bar, usually made commercially. Throughout the Caucasus and Central Asia, a version of it is also made at home. In areas of bee culture, pure honey is used instead of sugar syrup.

SERVINGS: 6–8 bars

  ¾ *cup butter (1½ sticks)*
  2 *cups flour*
  ¾ *cup sugar*
  2 *Tb water*
  ½ *cup coarsely chopped walnuts or almonds (optional)*

Melt butter, add flour, and stir until mixture is a thick paste. Continue cooking over a low fire 25–35 minutes, stirring frequently to keep the mass browning slowly and evenly. The use of an asbestos pad under the saucepan will reduce the amount of stirring needed. When the mixture is a light caramel color, bring sugar and water to boil in a separate saucepan and boil until the syrup will form a thin thread at the end of a spoon dipped in the pot and held vertically over it. Pour the syrup into the cooked butter and flour, add the chopped nuts (optional), stir to blend thoroughly and immediately pour the mass onto a large flat plate or marble slab. Press it into a thick rectangle with a knife and cut it in bars before it cools completely.

APPENDIX AND INDEX

BEVERAGES

TEA is the most popular Russian beverage. Usually served in glasses rather than cups, it is drunk in quantities at all times of day. Jam sometimes replaces sugar, and in Central Asia, the tea may be spiced with cloves and honey. Lithuanians are fond of teas made from garden herbs such as mint, or from caraway seed, to which they attribute curative powers.

Like Americans, Lithuanians drink milk with their meals. The usual beverage in the hot season in Armenia is tahn (yogurt diluted in water), similar to the Uzbek summer beverage of airan (sour milk diluted with water).

In the Ukraine, tea is traditionally served with a light supper of cold meats; other meals are more often accompanied by wines. Because only the southern part of the Ukraine is suitable for grape-growing, the wines of the north are homemade fruit wines. Currant wine is particularly popular, as is apple wine and apple-honey wine. Honey is used by both Ukrainians and Lithuanians to make a stronger beverage—mead, and in every rural Ukrainian community in America there is still someone making mead for himself and his friends according to the old recipes. Ukrainians also used to make homemade beer in addition to the popular Russian kvass, a mildly alcoholic drink of fermented rye bread that was every Russian's way of using up old rye crusts.

Georgia is famous for its wines. There are vineyards in Azerbaidzhan, Uzbekistan, Turkmenia, and the Crimea, too. Brandies are made as well as champagnes and table wines of all kinds, but by far the most popular strong liquor throughout Russia is vodka.

Vodka traditionally accompanies zakusky, and many Russians continue drinking vodka throughout the meal. Vodka is served ice cold in small glasses, shot-glass size. The glass is supposed to be drained in one gulp, preceded by a toast and immediately followed by a bite of food. Sipping, the theory goes, is more intoxicating. Vodka is sold in various strengths: 80 or 100 proof is the usual, although stronger vodkas are made. The flavors vary too. One of the most popular is zubrovka, vodka flavored with an herb translated in English as "buffalo grass." Less usual is the fiery pertsovka, vodka with a strong pepper infusion. Orange and lemon vodkas have more appeal for most people. Both are easy to prepare from ordinary vodka.

ORANGE VODKA

Wash an orange, cut the peel in a long thin strip, put the strip in the vodka, close the bottle, and leave it in the refrigerator about 24 hours. Remove peel and serve vodka.

NOTE: It is easy to remove the peel if you transfer the vodka to a wide-necked decanter or carafe, tape the top of the peel to the neck of the carafe, and close the top with aluminum foil.

LEMON VODKA is made the same way, using a lemon instead of an orange.

SOUR MILK, SOUR CREAM, AND OTHER DAIRY PRODUCTS

THERE is a wide range of milks and creams throughout Russia—soured through natural processes, soured with the addition of various cultures, soured and fermented, baked, skimmed, boiled, clabbered—and all known by various names to various nationalities. There are alcoholic milk beverages (kumiss, the fermented mare's milk of the Central Asian herdsmen) and refreshing summer drinks. In addition, many sauces, stews, and soups depend on these milks and creams for their flavor. Some dishes, such as the herdsmen's recipes that require the first milk of a mare, are not easily reproduced, but they are not commonly encountered in Russia either. The essential milk products can be reduced to 4: sour milk, sour cream, yogurt, and cottage cheese.

The term "sour" is inadequate and unfortunate. "Soured" milk and cream, especially when freshly made, are not sour. Sour cream, or smetana, is one of the most important ingredients in Russian cooking. Fortunately it is very easy to make at home, and the result is a richer, sweeter, and thicker product than commercially soured cream (page 226).

Sour milk is the particular delight of Lithuanians. One of the most enjoyable dishes I have ever eaten was the first course in a Lithuanian restaurant: a hot boiled potato with a side dish of sour milk. It hardly sounds like an epicurean delight, but it was. The contrast of thick, rich, cool milk with the hot, nutty-flavored potato was delicious. Very poor Lithuanians used to make a meal of this and I think they are rather to be envied.

In Lithuania, milk is simply left in a saucer in a warm
spot overnight, eaten in the morning, and replaced.
There is always a saucer or two of milk in the cupboard,
either thickening or ready to eat. Best chilled after sour-
ing, the milk will keep about a week in the refrigerator;
thereafter it separates and becomes watery.

Homogenized milk, almost the only fresh milk available in the United States outside of a farming area,
usually remains thin and turns bitter when left to sour.
What is commercially labeled "approved" milk is not
homogenized and can be soured in the old way or with
the addition of a tablespoon of sour cream to help start
it, but the milk is not easy to obtain. Most people will
have to be content with a substitute. One Lithuanian
told me he mixes sour cream with milk, half and half.
Other substitutes are given on the following page.

Yogurt is generally available. In certain areas, there
may be a choice of brands. Some are thicker and less
sour than others, and these are worth seeking. The
cottage cheese Russians use, which they call tvorog, is a
dry one similar to our pot cheese. Ours is not as rich,
however. To make it more like the Russian, add 1 Tb
butter per 12-oz. carton; if it is extremely dry, stir in Tb
sour cream. Should pot cheese not be available, wrap
large curd creamed cottage cheese in cheesecloth or a
kitchen towel and press it under a heavy weight for
several hours to extract liquid.

SMETANA

Sour Cream

>   ½ pint heavy cream
>   2½ tsp buttermilk

Sterilize a glass container by putting it in a pan of water,
bringing the water to a boil, and leaving the container
in boiling water for 3 minutes. Drain the container.

Shake the pint of cream and pour half of it into the container. Shake a botle of buttermilk and add 2½ tsp to the cream. Pour in remaining cream, close container, and leave it in a warm place 12–24 hours or until it thickens. Chill it thoroughly in the refrigerator before using.

SOUR-MILK SUBSTITUTE #1

SERVINGS: 4 cups

  3 cups thick buttermilk
  1 cup sour cream

Let buttermilk stand until it separates. Pour off the thin liquid. Mix 3 cups of the remaining thick liquid with 1 cup sour cream. Chill before using.

SOUR-MILK SUBSTITUTE #2

SERVINGS: 4 cups

  1 cup yogurt
  1 cup sour cream
  2 cups cold water

Mix well and chill before using.

SUGGESTIONS FOR USE OF LEFTOVER DOUGH

WRAPPED in wax paper and placed in a plastic bag, almost all doughs can be kept several days in the refrigerator and much longer in a freezer. Let dough come to room temperature and blend again before using.

Leftover sweet dough can be used for sweet vatrushky (small tarts, made following the recipe for Vatrushka on page 208), for fruit tarts with any fruit pie filling, or for sugar cookies.

To make sugar cookies, roll out dough about ¼" thick, cut it with a glass 2"–3" or more in diameter, sprinkle the rounds with sugar, and bake them on a greased sheet in a 375° oven 10–15 minutes or until they are beginning to turn brown and slide easily on the surface of the sheet.

Because the doughs for pirozhky, kulebiaka, and soup vatrushky are interchangeable, you can make one with leftover dough from the other. You can also achieve variety by using a different stuffing. For example, if you have made pirozhky with meat stuffing, you might make more pirozhky with cabbage or mushroom filling. Pirozhky and vatrushky, once baked, can always be frozen for later use.

TABLE OF EQUIVALENT MEASUREMENTS AND OVEN TEMPERATURES

a pinch	less than ⅛ teaspoon
3 teaspoons (tsp)	1 tablespoon (Tb)
16 tablespoons	1 cup
2 cups	1 pint
2 liquid cups	1 pound (lb.)
16 ounces (oz.)	1 pound
2 pints	1 quart (qt.)
4 cups	1 quart
4 quarts	1 gallon
½ cup or 8 tablespoons butter	¼ pound butter
½ cup or 8 tablespoons cream cheese	¼ pound cream creese
1 cup pot cheese	6 ounces
3 medium potatoes	1 pound potatoes

OVEN TEMPERATURES

very slow	225° F.
slow	275° F.
moderate	350° F.
hot	400° F.
very hot	475° F.

GLOSSARY OF FOREIGN TERMS AND SPECIAL INGREDIENTS

airan   Uzbek summer beverage of sour milk diluted in water

baba   a tall, cylindrical cake of yeast dough made by Ukrainians at Easter

bakhlava   a Near Eastern many-layered pastry; sometimes spelled pakhlava

barberis   *see* barberry

barberry   a berry dried, powdered, and used as a condiment in the Caucasus, Central Asia, and the Middle East; sold in Armenian and Near Eastern groceries under the names barberis or sumakh

basterma   dried beef seasoned with hot peppers and fenugreek; popular in the Caucasus; sometimes spelled pasterma

bekmes   grape syrup; a sweetish sauce used on meats in the Caucasus and sold at Armenian and Near Eastern groceries in America

beoreg   usually refers to a many-layered stuffed and baked Armenian pastry; can also mean a stuffed vegetable

bitky   meat balls

blinchiky   Russian pancakes of thin, unleavened batter

bliny   Russian pancakes, almost always yeast-raised

borshch   generally a beet soup made from meat bouillon and rendered tart by the addition of kvass, lemon juice, or vinegar

borshchok a meat-stock borshch in which beets are the sole vegetable

Brindza cheese a white cheese used in many parts of Eastern Europe and resembling the feta cheese of Greece and the Near East in flavor; sold in some specialty shops in America

chikhirtma usually refers to a soup thickened with egg yolks and popular in the Caucasus and Central Asia, although a main dish made of sautéed boneless chicken or lamb topped with eggs and baked in the oven is also called chikhirtma

coriander fresh coriander is very popular in the Caucasus; not widely sold in the United States, it can sometimes be found in Puerto Rican or Mexican groceries; substitute ground dried coriander or coriander seeds if fresh is not available

dolma a stuffed food, usually a vegetable stuffed with meat and rice (Caucasian)

fenugreek an Asiatic herb with aromatic seeds, ground and sold in Armenian and Near Eastern groceries under the name chaimen

feta cheese a white cheese sold in America and resembling the white cheeses popular in the various regions of the Caucasus; submerged in salt brine, feta cheese can be kept for months in the refrigerator; unless cheese is sold in a jar with brine, it is advisable to bring a jar and ask for some of the brine when buying feta

filo dough paper-thin leaves of dough used in making the many-layered Caucasian, Middle Eastern, and Greek pastries, and in the strudels of Eastern Europe; sometimes called strudel dough; sold in Armenian, Greek, Near Eastern, East European, and

	some German and Austrian groceries, and in certain supermarkets
gora	small undeveloped grapes left on the vine after the harvest (Caucasian)
grenky	grilled cheese toast
halva	a Near Eastern candy bar
hlodnik	*see* kholodnik
kasha	a dry porridge of any grain; buckwheat (grechnevaya kasha) is the most common
kazmag	a flat bread of unleavened egg dough put at bottom of casserole in making Azerbaidzhani pilaf
kebab	barbecued (Caucasian)
keufta	meat ball or meat patty (Caucasian)
kholodnik	general term for cold soups (Ukrainian, Lithuanian)
kilky	Kiel sprats (small fish from the Baltic Sea), imported in America in cans
kissel	usually a purée of tart fruit thickened with potato starch, although the name can be used for milk and other puddings
kizil	Cornelian cherry; native to the Caucasus where it is made into a syrup used on shashlik
klukva	a variety of cranberry native to northern Russia and the Baltic area
kotlety	cutlet or chop; usually refers to ground meat fried in the shape of a cutlet
krupenik	barley soup
kulebiaka	a large covered pastry filled with meat, vegetables, or fish
kulich	a kind of coffee cake traditionally served at Easter in Russia
kumiss	a beverage of fermented mare's milk, popular in the steppes of Central Asia
kvass	a mildly alcoholic drink usually made of fermented rye and used as a beverage and in certain soups, principally borshch and okroshka; a fermented liquid made from

	beets and known as beet kvass is sometimes used in borshch instead of rye kvass
kyurdyuk	fat taken from under the tails of lambs of a species bred in the Caucasus and Central Asia; the fat is used in cooking in those areas
lapsha	noodles
lobio	kidney beans (Georgian)
lukhum	a Near Eastern candy
manty	large stuffed dumplings of Central Asia and parts of the Caucasus
Maslyanitsa	the week preceding Lent; the name comes from maslo, the Russian word for butter
mezza	Armenian assorted appetizers
mint	dried mint, sold in Armenian and Near Eastern groceries, is crushed and used on soups and certain dishes; fresh mint can be washed and dried by hanging it in an airy place in a bag of cheesecloth; when dry it should be stored in air-tight containers
misof	meat and vegetable stew (Armenian)
nalysnyky	pancakes made with thin butter (Ukrainian)
narsharab	a sourish syrup of cooked pomegranate juice from pressed fruit and seeds; sold in Armenian and Near Eastern groceries
okroshka	a cold soup, usually made with kvass and raw vegetables combined with meat or fish
oladky	thick pancakes
ouha or *oukha*	a clear soup, usually of fish
pakhlava	*see* bakhlava
paramach	small Tartar meat pies
paska	an elaborately decorated cake made by Ukrainians for Easter
paskha	cottage cheese dessert made by Russians for Easter

pasterma	see basterma
pelmeny	stuffed dumplings
pertsovka	vodka infused with pepper
pilaf	long grain rice cooked in the Near Eastern manner and served combined with other ingredients
pilau	see pilaf
pir	old Slavic word for feast
pirog	large covered pastry
pirozhky	plural of pirozhok
pirozhnoye	pastry in general
pirozhok	a small turnover with a savory filling
piti	a popular Azerbaidzhani lamb soup, traditionally prepared in small, individual earthenware casseroles
plov	see pilaf
poppy seed	used extensively in baking in Lithuania and the Ukraine, poppy seed is sold in bulk in German and East European specialty shops
raki	alcoholic beverage of the Near East
sesame seed paste	ground sesame seeds, also known as sesame tahini or taheeni and sold in Near Eastern and Oriental groceries and specialty shops
shashlik	meat roasted on a skewer
shchav	sorrel soup
shchavel	sorrel
shchi	a meat stock soup of green vegetables; cabbage is usually the principal ingredient sour shchi: sauerkraut soup; green shchi: sorrel and spinach soup
shish kebab	meat roasted on a spit (shish = skewer; kebab = barbecued)
sirnichky	Ukrainian cottage cheese patties
smetana	sour cream
sumakh	see barberry
suris	Lithuanian white cheese

taheeni or *tahini*	*see* sesame seed paste
tahn	Armenian summer beverage of yogurt diluted in water
targhana or *trahana*	dried yogurt dough used in Armenian soup called Targhana; the dough is sold in packages in Armenian groceries
tchadi	Georgian corn bread
tushi	Armenian vegetable pickles
tvorog	Russian dry cottage cheese (similar to our pot cheese)
tvorozhniky	Russian cottage cheese patties
ushky	tiny dumplings, made like Siberian pelmeny, but smaller, and served in soups
vareniky	Ukrainian stuffed dumplings
vatrushka	a cheese pastry
vatrushky	plural of vatrushka; usually small cottage cheese tarts served with soup
vine leaves	sold bottled in many specialty shops and groceries
virtiniai	Lithuanian dumplings
wheat, cracked	bulgur wheat, sold in packages in some groceries and in bulk at Armenian and Near Eastern specialty shops where it is numbered from 1 to 3 according to the degree of coarseness
zakusits	to have a snack
zakuska	an appetizer or hors d'oeuvre
zakusky	plural of zakuska; Russian assorted appetizers
zirvak	braised meat and vegetable mixture which is the base for most Uzbek pilafs
zrazy	meat roulades
zubrovka	an herb known in English as buffalo grass; also vodka in which that herb has been steeped

WHERE TO OBTAIN
SPECIAL INGREDIENTS

IF you live in a city of any size, there is probably a neighborhood where many people of Slavic birth live and a number of small shops that carry Russian specialty foods such as *cracked wheat* and *buckwheat; special honeys* such as *linden or raspberry; black rye bread, babka* and other *pastries; caviar* and *smoked fish,* such as *sturgeon* or *sprats; halva* and other *sweets; pirozhky* and *pelmeny.* In New York City this locality is, roughly, the Lower East Side between East Eighth and Essex Streets, and it includes these shops:

Babka Pastries
60 East Eighth Street

*Russ and Daughters
179 East Houston Street

*Gormet Appetizers, Inc.
203 East Houston Street

*M. Schacht
99 Second Avenue

Ratner's Bake Shop
115 Second Avenue

*Myron Surmach
11 East Seventh Street

Products such as *feta and brindza cheese, bekmes* and *narsharab; barberis, fenugreek, sesame-seed paste, dried mint* and other Caucasian *herbs* or *spices; targhana;* and *vine leaves,* can be found in Armenian or Near Eastern groceries, which in New York City cluster around Third and Lexington Avenues in the Twenties. Three of the best of these shops are:

*House of Yemen East
370 Third Avenue

*K. Kalustyan
123 Lexington Avenue

*Karnig Tashjian
380 Third Avenue

Feta and other *cheeses* can also be found in New York's Greek groceries such as:

Athens Food Market   *Kassos Brothers
542 Ninth Avenue   570 Ninth Avenue
                            ($10.00 minimum mail order)

Filo dough is sometimes stocked by the last five shops, or may be ordered from:

*Constantinople Oriental Pastry Shop
348 Eighth Avenue
(2 pounds minimum mail order)

*Cappello's Imported Foods
5328 Lemmon Avenue
Dallas, Texas
    (who also stock a
    number of other Russian
    or Near Eastern products)

NOTE: *Cracked wheat, buckwheat kasha, caviar, smoked fish* of various kinds, *feta cheese, vine leaves* and *filo dough* are items often carried by gourmet shops of all nationalities.

---

* Starred sources can fill orders by mail.

INDEX

ABOUT THE AUTHOR

Born in a Chicago suburb, BARBARA NORMAN was
graduated from Stanford University in Russian studies
and then worked and lived in Washington, D. C.,
Munich and Paris. She resigned from the U.S. Embassy
in Paris in 1957 after her marriage to concert violinist
Paul Makanowitzky, who is of Russian origin. She has
since translated several Russian classics into English for
publication under her married name while moving between Paris, Spain and New York. She is the author of
The Spanish Cookbook (1966), a selection of The
Cookbook Guild.

SOUP'S ON!

AMERICA'S FAVORITE RECIPES FROM BETTER HOMES & GARDENS. From appetizers to luscious desserts —over 500 prize-tested recipes—275 photographs!
(NE4578—95¢)

HAWAII COOKBOOK & BACKYARD LUAU by Elizabeth Ahn Toupin. 175 succulent recipes plus tempting menu suggestions to turn your kitchen into an exotic tropical paradise!
(SE13—75¢)

James Beard's HORS D'OEUVRES & CANAPES. Great for party-giving success—sizzling taste treats and cool bite-size delights.
(SE4384—75¢)

THE ART OF BARBECUE COOKING. What to cook on— what to cook with—full-color photographs of many appetizing dishes—plus a special chapter on sauces.
(NE4782—95¢)

THE FANNIE FARMER JUNIOR COOKBOOK by Wilma Lord Perkins. The famous, illustrated guide that's been the favorite of young cooks for over two decades. (SE4677—75¢)

THE COMPLETE BOOK OF MEXICAN COOKING by Elisabeth Ortiz. 340 delicious recipes in the most complete and colorful guide to Mexican cooking ever written.
(NE4107—95¢)

THE SPANISH COOKBOOK by Barbara Norman. Precise and simple directions for over 200 of the best recipes from the kitchens of Spain.
(SE4389—75¢)

AN HERB AND SPICE COOKBOOK by Craig Clairborne. The food editor of *The New York Times* presents over 400 original and tempting recipes, prepared with dozens of different herbs and spices—a subtle choice of the finest cuisine throughout the world.
(NE5427—95¢)

Ask for them at your local bookseller or use this handy coupon: